# FOREWORD

Roy Blatchford has produced a highly rea‹
volume on Good Governance, which cou‹
not just by governors, members and trus
education sector. Indeed, most or all of the advice and lesson
be of value to governors and trustees in the world beyond education -
both in business and charities contexts.

Too often, governance is seen or treated as a 'tick box' add on, and
something which requires limited specific skills or reflection to do well.

But delivering really good – or preferably 'great' – governance is rare, and
does not happen by accident. Governing bodies need to be more than
ineffective 'rubber stamps'. Too often, executive teams are not properly
but respectfully held to account. And too often governors will feel that
their skills and commitment are not being fully utilised.

This volume distils many decades of experience and observation in
English education and from overseas and provides both accessible and
useful guidance about good practice, but also a lot of thought-provoking
examples of the types of challenges that have to be addressed by chairs,
governors and executive teams.

Good – and Great – governance has a key role to play in tackling current
education challenges, driving improvements in standards and limiting
risks. But it has attracted too little thought and reflection from policymakers and too little in the way of accessible advice for practitioners.
This book plays an important part in filling that gap.

**David Laws**
**Minister of State for Schools, 2012–2015, School Governor.**

# INTRODUCTION

Why an A–Z on governance? Governance is as simple as ABC. And yet it is not.

The truth is that good governance lies at the heart of all great organisations, whether in the private, public or not-for-profit sectors. Scratch any business, charity, trust, school, college, university or government department just a little and whether there is secure and strong governance quickly surfaces.

Over the past 40 years I have worked up close with governors, trustees, directors and members in the education and charity sectors. When lexicographer Dr Samuel Johnson was asked, 'What is poetry?' he replied, 'It is easier to say what it is not'. So with governance: when governance is confident and competent, the organisation it oversees flows smoothly. When governance falters, the reverberations are quickly felt – and tend to attract adverse publicity in the blink of an eye.

In sporting parlance, at the end of a game of hockey or rugby, if no one has even mentioned or noticed the referee, you can be reasonably sure that the proceedings have been well managed. It's when the referee's actions become the story, you know that not all has passed without question. Good governance in action passes almost without comment, yet its inner workings are far from simple.

This A–Z seeks to capture the essence of positive and successful governance in schools, colleges and trusts as I have seen it practised in the UK and overseas. My favoured approach of 'less is more', cutting to the heart of a subject, means trying to capture in just a few pages a particular aspect of governance crucial to success. Deliberately, there are overlapping and complementary themes and key words. Leadership matters permeate.

The book is aimed unashamedly at that dynamic partnership of *those who govern* and *those who are governed*: provocation, reflection and guidance for school, college and trust leaders; and for the many, many thousands of volunteers who give generously of their time sitting on governing boards of all descriptions in a kindly watchdog spirit. British volunteerism – 'civic giving' if you will – is writ large in these contexts across the nation.

In common with all titles in the series (see page 200), Section One is organised around the 26 letters of the English alphabet. The narrative is both macro and micro, from setting the strategy to the minutiae of effective meetings. We move from **A**mbassador and **D**elegation, through **M**inutes and **N**olan, to **W**alkabout and **Y**outh. In the spirit of challenging assumptions, letters **Y** and **Z** have been switched for a purpose.

The **ASIDES: What to do?**, which round off each chapter, present real, lively governance scenarios that focus on challenging situations. Thinking through resolutions to these scenarios takes the reader to the heart of good governance.

Section Two includes a variety of material for further training and discussion, alongside 'best practice' documentation on governance culled from different sources.

In writing this book, I have held in mind so many colleagues with whom I have collaborated and from whom I have learned over the years. That education continues. My warm thanks to them.

May good governance go among you.

**Roy Blatchford**

## A note on nomenclature in this book

In the world of educational governance, the following words are current (in this book lower case is used throughout):

**governor:** the word commonly applied to those who sit on governing bodies in schools.

**trustee:** the word usually applied to those who sit on multi-academy trust boards, created as charities.

**director/non-executive:** the words commonly applied to those who are 'company directors', a part of the contemporary trust landscape.

**board member:** two words that are applied to encompass any of the above.

**Members:** (with a capital M) essentially guardians of the trust who appoint trustees. The mystery of the Members is explored on page 9.

**multi-academy trusts:** the trustees of the academy trust are both charity trustees and company directors.

The Academy Trust Handbook 2024 (Education and Skills Funding Agency, 2024) is *the* handbook for governors and trustees. It identifies (a) requirements and (b) minimum good practice within the national framework. It is regularly updated.

# CONTENTS

**Section Two**

# ABOUT THE AUTHOR

Roy Blatchford is founder of www.blinks.education, which works with schools, local authorities, academy trusts, colleges and universities in the UK and internationally. Roy was founder (2006-16) of the National Education Trust and previously served as one of Her Majesty's Inspectors of Schools (HMI) in England. He has inspected and reviewed over 1000 schools and colleges in Europe, the US, the Middle East and India. For three years he implemented education system reform in the Gulf Region.

Roy has spent much of his personal and professional life serving on more than 30 boards – in the health and prison services, in social care and the arts – and continues to chair leaders, governors and trustees in the education and charity sectors. He was appointed CBE for services to education in the 2016 New Year Honours.

Roy is author of *The A–Z of Great Classrooms* (Blatchford, 2023) and editor of the A–Z series.

*To my mother, Barbara Mary Blanche Blatchford,*
*100 not out in January 2025 – a lifelong volunteer.*

# SECTION ONE

# AMBASSADORS

**Good governors and trustees are powerful ambassadors for their organisations and communities.**

Sir Ken Morrison, founder of the supermarket chain, called a spade a spade. Following his death, stories of his bluff Yorkshire nature have been legion. At one of the retailer's annual meetings in his native Bradford, he launched a verbal assault on the then chief executive, Dalton Philips, from which Mr Philips would not recover.

'When I left work and started working as a hobby, I chose to raise cattle', the veteran grocer boomed. 'I have something like 1,000 bullocks and, having listened to your presentation, Dalton, you've got a lot more bull**** than me.' (Neville, 2014).

Sir Ken eschewed the world of the City and corporate governance edicts. Memorably, he once asked why have non-executive directors when he could have checkout assistants instead. And he was never happier than when pacing stores, weaving through the aisles talking to staff and shoppers, and working out what was selling well, what was not, and why.

Reading of Sir Ken's style and relationship with his chief executives set me thinking how I, as a headteacher/principal in different contexts, have interacted over the years with chairs of governors.

School leaders know, in sickness and in health, that *the* critical factor in running a successful school is a flourishing professional relationship with the chair of governors or trustees. A head who does not view the chair as their boss usually comes unstuck. The chair may well have been the person who had the final say in your appointment, so they are rooting for you to succeed.

As a young teacher in large London comprehensives during the 1970s, I was aware of two distinguished chairs of governors: Lord Mishcon at Stockwell Manor and Sir Ashley Bramall at Pimlico School. To me they were distant figures with splendid white hair, glimpsed going into the head's office for important meetings or listened to keenly on annual speech days.

To everyone on the staffs they were outstanding ambassadors for comprehensive education in the Inner London Education Authority (ILEA) – much needed in those heady political times.

Only later in my career, interviewing the heads they worked with, did I discover just how much time and personal support Lord Mishcon and Sir Ashley gave regularly, despite their own demanding professional duties in the law and local government. Those were the days of disruptive teacher union action, community tensions in the estates, stop-and-search on Brixton's streets, and IRA bomb threats to schools.

Moving in 1982 as deputy to a North London grammar school going comprehensive, I encountered a set of Camden and Highgate governors not to be messed with. Their combined legal, academic and financial acumen was formidable, nay, intimidating. And then Sir Peter Newsam (retiring ILEA chief) joined the board.

For my term as acting head, their patience with the rookie head was invaluable. When the really sticky moment came of having to deal with the suspension of a member of staff (who also happened to be a magistrate), the chair was unfailing in helping me follow due procedures – affording timely counsel when I doubted my own abilities. Above all, I learned that the very best of governors are *privately critical and publicly loyal* – probably *the* most important lesson for headteachers and principals in their dealings with boards.

****

There were two outstanding chairs of governors during my headship days: Robert Palmer and Chris Pym. I think it no coincidence that their peers nominated them, for both were likeable, intelligent, compassionate men. The former appointed me in Oxfordshire, the latter in Milton Keynes – both invested in me from the days we first met.

Robert Palmer was a senior officer in Thames Valley Police. Working with him for a decade was the most pleasurable professional relationship I ever enjoyed in a school. His ability to judge people whom he had only just met and to assess the merits of any situation were remarkable. On interview panels his dry humour used to keep everyone gently in order and constantly amused.

He taught me that guiding, creative principle of leadership: it's easier to beg forgiveness than seek permission. It suited us both that he was adept at keeping his distance from the school to let me get on with things. Equally, he was always there at the end of the phone: to offer advice the day a sixth former took his own life by hanging, and on the occasion when the British National Party came leafleting students at the school gate.

He also possessed a personal bank of sayings which he had honed well over his years in the police force: 'The grass elsewhere is greener, until you have mown it a few times'; 'If you stand still long enough, you become a radical'; 'Graveyards are full of indispensable people'. He would quote these at moments in meetings to offer pinpoint summaries of discussions, so we could judiciously move on.

Of course Robert had his foibles. He was always the *Chairman*; chairs, he asserted, were for sitting on. And lighting up a favourite cigar while standing by the finishing tape on sports days used to wind up the head of PE wonderfully!

Chris Pym appointed me to open a brand-new school and learning centre – in state-of-the-art premises – which he wished to be both traditional and radical in practice and outlook. That suited 1999, on the cusp of a new century, and both our temperaments and educational intuitions. His political nous, deep knowledge of community, adroit handling of founding governors with different agendas, passion for deep learning and out-of-the-box thinking were everything the founding staff team and student body required to shape a sustainable vision.

For a few short years we chose to meet every Monday afternoon for a couple of hours in the school's café. This was a statement to staff about our partnership and provided me with a regular opportunity to sound out my latest brilliant ruse. 'Don't scare the horses', he would say, knowing how experimental we could and couldn't be with parents who wanted the best of a Buckinghamshire grammar school blended with a pioneering comprehensive.

Chris's sudden death through rapidly progressive cancer hit me hard. At his memorial service I recognised his family had lost a venerated father figure of many parts. I had lost a founding partner.

The words he expressed at one of our weekly discussions stay with me. I can hear him still: 'Never name a building after anyone living or dead. With the living, you never know what they will get up to. With the dead, imagine what skeletons might be uncovered'. It is *his* imprint much more than mine that lives on in that school community today.

\*\*\*\*

Reflecting further on what the chairs of governors with whom I worked closely brought to their respective roles, places and points in time, in common with Sir Ashley and Lord Mishcon, they were each outstanding *ambassadors* for comprehensive education, in every thoughtful word and deed.

When the schools they served came in for unfair criticism from parents, press or local politicians with axes to grind, they were unfailingly polite and firm in their responses. They were equally open to and accepting of fair critiques – so important in a community leader.

Furthermore, each was determinedly optimistic in their dealings with staff, students and families. They believed in the missions of the schools and what teachers and students were seeking to achieve together. That optimism was infectious and was critically important to both the school and local community.

So I applaud these chairs of governors for their distinguished voluntary service and their vital role in my own education as a headteacher. I commend their wise words and thoughts to the current generation of school leaders.

# ASIDE

## WHAT TO DO?

In good faith, one of the governors has used his very good contacts in business to secure a substantial financial gift to the school's fundraising appeal for a new sports hall. He presents a short paper which gathers great support. A press release is sent to local media.

Two weeks later, it emerges that the gift is coming from a company that has investments in products which promote quite the opposite of healthy living. Staff and students have been discussing the matter and taken sides in quite unhelpful ways.

*The governing board meets to discuss its response...*

\*\*\*\*

There have been a series of leaks of confidential information from governors' meetings. The most recent brought into the public domain a sensitive staffing matter, which the person concerned has taken to her professional association.

The board has received a letter from the professional association requesting an external review of these leaks. An initial discussion by the board is fraught and indecisive. A special meeting is arranged.

*The governing board meets to explore next steps...*

\*\*\*\*

# BOARDS

**Effective boards skilfully weigh their
*oversight* and *insight* roles.**

General Sir Mike Jackson (1944-2024), former chief of the general staff, held every rank from officer cadet to four-star general. Of a stint at the Ministry of Defence in London he described that apparently humdrum role as being all about Bs: 'bands, belts, berets, badges, buttons, banners, bars (medals), bars (booze), burglary, bullying, barbiturates, bosoms, babies, bonking and buggery' (Rathbone, 2024).

Who needs Boards with a capital B? Looking back through the history books of England and the Empire (Board of Trade dating back to the 17th century is a notable one), it is evident that boards came into being in a wide variety of contexts and continue to be very much part of governance today across many sectors of our society. They were created to regulate, to approve, to nurture, to protect, to challenge, to restrain...in one phrase: *to afford oversight and insight.*

Boards in many commercial situations are made up of paid non-executive directors, while across the public service, boards comprise volunteers in the best British tradition of 'amateurism'. In French, interestingly, that translates to 'enthusiast'!

## THE MYSTERY OF THE MEMBERS

Having been prime minister, Harold Macmillan was appointed chancellor of Oxford University (1960-1986). When asked what did the chancellor actually *do*, he wittily replied: 'Without a Chancellor there can be no Vice-Chancellor.'

In a world of multi-academy trusts, the 'top tier' of governance is occupied by Members. They are similar to a company's shareholders.

The role of Members is to hold the trustees to account, to assure themselves that the governance of the trust is effective and that trustees are acting in accordance with the trust's charitable objects. Members are not involved in the day-to-day business of the trust, yet enjoy key powers including the appointment and removal of trustees and amending the memorandum and articles of association.

Ambiguously, it is possible (not desirable) for Members also to be trustees. In charity law, Members are the guardians of the trust; they should not interfere other than utterly decisively when the trust is at risk.

'*Quis custodiet ipsos custodes*?', asked the Roman poet Juvenal. Who inspects the inspectors? Who appoints the Members? It's a question worth probing in any and every context. Answers are various and often lead to more questions. But ask away if you are a trustee or a governor appointed by a trust board. Even dig into the archives, which can lead to fascinating trails…

## THE MIX

A board comprising volunteers is a many-splendoured thing. Look around you when you are next at a board meeting. How does each and every board come together? Who are the people and what are their skills? Do executive leaders get the governors they deserve? Do governors get the executive they deserve?!

One might reasonably surmise that contacts and address books feature in putting together a governing board. Advertisements and recruitment agencies also play their part. In the case of a new school coming into being, a shadow board is created with governors representing different local interests: the county, the district, parents, local community, religious groups.

With established schools, when a vacancy arises, incumbent governors may well be asked to nominate someone they think would make a significant contribution to governance ahead, and interviews will follow.

There are elections for parent governors from the parent body – elections which often need thoughtful management from the executive and chair.

With some boards, when vacancies arise a self-audit of current governors' skills will be conducted to glean where 'gaps' might exist. Many boards carry out a two-yearly self-audit, by way of keeping themselves under review.

There is no magic formula for putting together a group of volunteers who will provide and model good governance. Over time, as in any context, groups happily gel or not, and find out for themselves how best to get along – after all, it is the amateur tradition. Efforts over the years to professionalise governance through payment of chairs have foundered on the altar of that commitment to the volunteer tradition.

The wise, reflective board will look around its meeting table and seek to have a range of backgrounds, dispositions and skills among its number. Whether members spend their days looking after a family, running a business or working in the public, private or not-for-profit sector, when they come together as governors they are unequivocally there to be ambassadors, champions and guardians of the school, college or trust.

What is fascinating and pleasurable to watch over time on a board – and through important committee work – is how governors learn to appreciate each other's strengths, build relationships, grow in confidence to challenge another's viewpoints, gently tolerate individual idiosyncrasies and pet subjects – and, importantly, know when to move in a united way when difficult decisions are required. As one long-serving chair puts it: 'We unite, all differences intact'.

## OVERSIGHT

There are clearly set out responsibilities for governors and trustees (see examples in Section Two). Multi-academy trust models of governance vary.

In essence, if you are called a 'governor' or a 'trustee' your formal responsibilities are pretty much the same – rooted in charity, education, health and safety, and other laws – wherever you are in the country. Local interpretation of national policy has always been a feature of

UK governance, whether in education, housing, health or roads. In international contexts, the rules and regulations may differ.

Documents (electronic or paper, ask for which you prefer) outline a plethora of finance, safety, wellbeing and education matters, which, frankly, can feel quite daunting. Governors will take time to read key documents and regular updates, and can reasonably expect to be taken through, page by page, vital policies. A number of boards divide up the many policies and ask each governor to have a special eye on two or three, working with a member of the executive – an efficient and successful practice.

What does all this amount to? The key word is *oversight*. There is a paid executive team to ensure policies are put fairly and safely into practice. Governors are there to lift the carpet where they sense it needs lifting; to interrogate a particular practice where that is required; to approve changes and modifications as appropriate; and to commend when commendation is deserved.

Former US President, Bill Clinton, and the election team which took him into office in 1993 used to talk about KISS: Keep it Simple Stupid. A confident chair will give governors and trustees a similar steer in relation to oversight: keep the big picture in mind, delve into the detail as required, speak as you find, challenge complacency, affirm agreement in the best interests of the children, young people and staff we serve.

# INSIGHT

Vitally, governors bring their personal and professional experiences to the board and committees, each time they meet. The oversight role – carefully scrutinising policies and procedures – is half the job. The other is bringing *insights* to the table, again rooted in life experiences. In two words: *be brave* as you do this.

There is significant merit in asking seemingly obvious questions, not to trip up school leaders but to encourage them to question often long-standing, nay tired practices:

- Why do you do things in this way?
- Have you thought about a different approach?

- Has it always been done like this?
- What does this cost?
- When was this last put out to tender?

It is the case in every walk of life that we who live something every day cannot see it afresh, and sometimes need to.

- We line the students up outside the building. Why?
- We have tutor period first thing in the morning. Why?
- The early years classrooms have always been in the old portacabins. Why?
- The sixth-form common room shares the library. Do they have to?
- The buses have to leave by 3.30pm. Do they?

(See *A Guide to Blinks* (Blinks Education, 2025) for a fresh way of looking at schools and classrooms.)

It is always important for governors to challenge orthodoxies, even if that is then to find out why something is as it is. As a board member, you are bringing – without fear or favour – your intelligence and insights to the table.

And, just sometimes, executive leaders need to be reminded that they may not have all the solutions, that their judgement has not been quite right on this occasion, that to bend to a different approach is worth doing – it is point 10 below!

## THE ESSENCE OF A GREAT BOARD

*Reflecting on outstanding boards in action, thoughtfully balancing oversight and insights, what do we see?*

1. Deep care and interest in the school/trust from all board members.
2. A diverse, complementary set of skills.
3. Positive, optimistic mindsets, tempered by pragmatism.
4. Keen listeners, thoughtful talkers.
5. Strong awareness of risks and opportunities.
6. High quality documents circulated in a timely manner.

7. All members' command of documents circulated.
8. Well-judged links between main board and committees.
9. Skilled chairing and outstanding minuting.
10. Critique in private. Loyalty in public.

# ASIDE

## WHAT TO DO?

In a large secondary school, the people committee of the board wants to make additional investments in staffing for special educational needs. The recommendations are well argued, and the topic has appeared on a number of consecutive agendas.

A parent Facebook group has been campaigning for the school to meet a wider range of special educational needs, especially because partner primaries have been doing a very good job with meeting individual needs.

The finance and audit committee is increasingly alarmed by the financial implications for next year's budget. The principal has found herself in a difficult position, having made commitments to families that extra resources will be found.

*She asks the board for a way forward. . .*

\*\*\*\*

The chair of the school board has been in post for a decade, consistently re-elected because of his excellent leadership. He is a highly respected member of the village community.

Sadly, his health has deteriorated sharply in recent months. A couple of trusted governors have spoken privately to him on the matter, suggesting he stands down. He shows no signs of so doing.

*Who does what by way of next steps?. . .*

\*\*\*\*

# CHAIRS

**The professional understanding between the chair and the executive leader is arguably *the* decisive factor in the success of an organisation.**

A fondly-remembered English football manager, Graham Taylor, when at Watford FC, was asked what he wanted from a chairman. He half-seriously replied: 'Someone with lots of money and who is very busy in other directions.' Fortunately for Taylor, that chairman was the singer Elton John, and the friendship they developed over many years is well documented.

Taylor's response about being otherwise occupied may or may not be what most school leaders would give when asked what they want of their chair today, but it's a question worth pondering.

Does the chair restrain and temper the paid leader? Does the leader restrain and encourage the chair? Where does the balance lie?

## WHAT'S THE JOB DESCRIPTION?

*We are seeking a new chair to oversee a critical period of growth and development and lead an exceptionally capable and committed board. You will be a confident and positive leader and ambassador, with the strategic acumen and emotional intelligence to … etc.*

Are teachers born or made? Are chairs of governors born or made? Are some governors destined to become chairs? What's the process? Why become a chair? What are the rewards and downsides? What are the motives and motivation?

In common with teachers and school and trust leaders, chairs vary in quality. The very best make an enormous difference. The regular ones acquit themselves of their duties. And to be frank, when schools and trusts falter, the chair of governors/trustees may be part of the problem and may need to step down with dignity in everyone's best interests. See Lorenzetti (pp. 73–77).

Chairs of boards can come from within or outside the organisation. There are times when a school or trust will consider that an external appointment is timely and important for the development of good governance. The recruitment and appointment process which follows will doubtless involve current members of the board and take into account the views of the executive.

The external appointment is by its very nature seen as more of a risk by current board members – but they should have faith in their initial judgement to advertise externally and then in a careful appointment process. We are talking again here about unremunerated posts, albeit with important responsibilities to lead.

The internal appointment is easier if there is, as is often the case, a consensus that a current member is ready and willing to be chair and who is seen as a natural successor to the incumbent chair. An independent view is usually worth seeking.

Whatever the route to the chair role, it is likely that first and foremost the person is viewed as both 'an authority' and 'in authority'. No one is ever in doubt about the significant time commitment a chair as a volunteer makes, and being both *in* and *an* authority means that investment in time never goes away.

The chair will be seen by fellow governors as a powerful advocate and ambassador for the organisation; they will be seen as someone who has or can develop a nuanced rapport with the executive team. Whether naturally extrovert or introvert (to use those short-hand terms), the chair will exercise careful judgement with a quiet or loud voice, with gravitas, with a sparkle in their eye and a smile on their face – in sum, they will enjoy the confidence of those around them. A golden thread of humour running through governors' meetings and activities is not to be sniffed at.

There is no recipe for guaranteed success, and if the chair is new to the role, as we all are at some point, the support and occasional forgiveness from colleagues is essential. In turn, the chair will grow into the position and come to take real pleasure in orchestrating fellow volunteers to be the best they can be in supporting and restraining the executive team.

And chairs should ensure they put themselves up for election on an annual basis, and in accepting re-election, seek some formal feedback.

## Between meetings: working with the leadership team

There is a sense in which the chair's role is perceived as there to chair meetings – it's in the name! Ask any school or trust leader and this is profoundly not the case. A successful board thrives on the interactions between the chair and executive leader between meetings, often in emails, which challenge thinking, ways of doing and actions the board might take ahead.

There is always follow up to a previous committee or main board; there are always questions which need addressing; there are occasions when governors overstep their role and need a gentle nudge; there are misconceptions and misinformation to be tackled.

There is the email to the chair which usually starts: 'Hope you are well', then:

- 'Have you time for a quick call?'
- 'I'm a bit worried about what the CEO has said in her report.'
- 'Have you seen what the local paper has said about one of our board members?'
- 'I know we agreed to be at main meetings in person, but can I dial in on this occasion?'
- 'Can you remind a couple of forgetful governors about their DBS requirements?'
- 'What line are we taking on the remuneration proposals?'

And so on…chairs must keep smiling, and role play the intermittent scowl.

What executive leaders say they most value between meetings is some moral support when dealing with tricky personnel issues, and frankness in private with the chair to help sort out a really challenging issues that may have arisen on which there is division amongst the board. Chairs certainly have a vital – arguably unique – part to play in helping leaders accept that they are not always right.

Building and sustaining the flourishing professional relationship between the chair and school/trust leader is a sine qua non of effective governance. Both parties need constantly to work at it – upon that secure relationship lies in no small part the success of the organisation. And therein lies the deep satisfaction of being a chair. There are inevitably moments when as a volunteer you may question the time commitment. Yet to be party to a school community's successes is something to be treasured.

## Before meetings

The chair, school/trust leader and clerk will want to ensure everyone involved knows when and where the next meeting is taking place, and does everyone have the right papers, pdf, etc.? There may be points of clarification arising from the CEO's report that board members seek from the chair.

In common with most successful meetings, the preparatory groundwork means there should be no surprises. Many chairs and CEOs/headteachers have a shared mantra of *no surprises* – and that remains wise advice.

## During meetings

What are the key *self-reminders* for the chair?

1. Make sure everyone knows at least the name of everyone else in the room.
2. Does everyone have the requisite files/paperwork, as distributed by the clerk?
3. Can we all see the slides clearly?
4. Can we hear each other against the drone of the air conditioning?
5. Am I clear in identifying which agenda item we are on, and the purpose of the item?

6. Are the 'summing-ups' – whoever does them – clear and balanced, and do we know what action points are minuted?

7. Are we clear how committees might be taking a matter forward?

8. Am I keeping to time?

9. Am I involving everyone in the room?

10. Do we depart feeling we have achieved something worthwhile and looking forward to the next meeting?

A number of chairs keep the above by their side/on their tablet during meetings, as a sort of aide-mémoire.

## After meetings

There are invariably loose ends for the chair and the executive to follow through on, and these should be done as promptly as possible. There are sometimes some upset feelings and offended sensibilities to be fielded, and these often land in the lap of the chair. Nettles must be grasped.

Then the draft minutes will arrive for the chair to sign off – insist these are done expeditiously, or you will have forgotten, no matter how fine your memory is. Courteous and appreciative notes from time to time to the clerk never go amiss.

The recording of board meetings is neither commonplace nor recommended, and if they were recorded – for posterity or other causes – unquestionably there would be protocols to be established. The recording of online committee meetings is an increasing feature, linked to automatic minute taking.

## CODA

When I observe on different boards a confident, trusted chair in action in meetings, what do I see?

- Enjoyment in the role, with excellent eye contact
- Expert timekeeping, never hurrying
- Strong command of subject
- Inclusive of all contributions
- Encouraging the least confident member

- Subduing, nicely, the over-talkative member
- Calling on the executive to speak, but not too much
- Grasping nettles, as required
- Uniting views towards a common position
- Leading applause for successes
- Thanking warmly and departing on time.

The philosopher Lao Tzu (5th century BCE, China) wrote: 'A leader is best when people barely know he exists. When his work is done, his aim fulfilled, they will say: we did it ourselves.' Most chairs when they leave a board do not look backwards, but enjoy being thanked and want to feel they have left the organisation in at least as thriving a state as when they joined it.

---

# ASIDE

## WHAT TO DO?

The academy trust lead on training for school governors is indefatigable and chases up governors when they have not attended courses. Two chairs of governors have complained to the trust board that this approach is alienating volunteers.

The trust board chair has discussed the issue with the CEO, but this has had little apparent effect. Indeed, there have been three high profile resignations in the past month from school governors.

*The trust board has this matter as a major agenda item. What follows here?...*

****

The local authority has indicated that it will 'sign off' the school's budget plan with a 0.5% deficit, on the condition that governors agree to manage the in-year budget deficit. Governors are brainstorming proposals to claw back the deficit position in year. The decisions made will need to satisfy the local authority, as well as governors, with a level of detail beyond existing processes.

---

Ideas on the table include all unplanned maintenance to be approved by governors, a recruitment freeze, costing out a support staff redundancy scheme and conducting a strategic analysis of total spend against the school's strategic objectives.

The senior leadership team have asked governors to support with their monitoring of those areas in the school suffering the most from absences and reliance on temporary teachers this term. The school needs to allocate link governors to where they are most needed, but without overstepping the mark and going beyond 'governance' and straying into 'management'.

*What next from the governors?...*

\*\*\*\*

# DELEGATION

**Practising proper levels of delegation lies at the heart of a thriving governing board.**

A celebrated French general was once tactlessly asked, after a famous victory, if it hadn't really been won by the second-in-command. The general thought for some time before answering: 'Maybe so. But one thing is certain. If the battle had been lost, I would have lost it'.

Delegation in the field of governance does not fortunately lead to such dramatic consequences, but securing and practising proper levels of delegation with clarity is vital. Which decisions can be delegated? Are committee terms of reference understood? To paraphrase US President Harry S. Truman: where does the buck stop?

## MODELS OF GOVERNANCE: AN ELEPHANT IN THE ROOM

For the many, many governors of local-authority-maintained schools across the country, there is continuing clarity about their roles and responsibilities – and most thrive upon them. 'If it ain't broke, why fix it?' is their proper cry.

For those governors who have been used to the maintained system and then find themselves in a multi-academy trust system, there have been inevitable changes.

Schemes of delegation – a requirement in law – have arguably neutered the historic role of the governor. One commonly held view is that in many instances 'governor' is now a misnomer, one of many misuses of language that has crept into the public sector. Just as 'invest' really means 'spend', 'governor' has come to mean 'adviser'.

The critique runs: in many multi-academy trusts, the local management of schools' initiatives from decades ago – which took decision making out of local authorities and placed them into individual schools – have been rolled back, and meaningful governance is vested entirely in the trust board and central trust staff.

Some trusts are explicit about this shift, creating 'Advisory Councils' or 'Local Partnerships' or 'Academy Forums'. Others continue with, arguably, the pretence of decision making at local level and use the term 'governing body', whereas 'advisory committee' would be more appropriate.

It certainly is now the case that many local 'governing bodies' generally have no say in budgeting, HR, premises and IT. They may be held accountable for educational performance, pupil and sports premiums, but without meaningful input into the deployment of resources to achieve the desired outcomes.

Critics of the academy model of governance conclude that local democracy has been eroded. The clock has been wound back by CEOs and boards of trustees due to a combination of wanting to maintain control, accountability and 'we know best'. And thus governors, in the dictionary definition sense (to direct, to control, to rule with authority) no longer govern.

It is argued equally that where multi-academy trusts have made a deliberate point to hold onto the best features of governing bodies within the maintained sector – and the schemes of delegation are well crafted and transparent – then across the country are to be found many models which are working well, and governors attest to that.

The debate and critique above highlight the importance of everyone involved in governance having a secure shared understanding of the schemes of delegation within which they are operating. The phrase in politics of 'being in office but not in power' can be heard by disgruntled governors. Where this unease and evident dissatisfaction with responsibilities exists, or is perceived to exist, chairs and executive leaders have prompt and important steps to take – or the matter festers.

Governors are one of the largest volunteer forces in the country. It matters that their roles and responsibilities are clear to all participants, and genuinely valued.

## DEPUTY CHAIR

Most trust boards and many governing bodies elect a deputy chair, renewable on an annual basis. Not only is that person able to step in to chair meetings as required but it affords the chair an often-needed sounding board when challenging financial or personnel issues emerge. The executive may be pushing one solution but if the chair is not sure, they can turn to their deputy for advice.

With the sheer volume of paperwork – papers, revised salary policies, new legal requirements, changes to safeguarding procedures, updated Department of Education (DfE) guidance – two minds are surely better than one. Sharing a chair's responsibilities makes great sense in contemporary governance. Succession planning is a further dimension. And a wise chair will always ask a deputy for honest feedback on how they chaired a meeting and dealt with a tricky issue – warts and all.

Co-chairs are also a feature of the educational landscape, less common, but if carefully established and practised with clarity of roles, they prove effective.

And – see page 5 – graveyards are full of indispensable people.

## COMMITTEES

To scan a range of trust and school schemes of delegation is to be met with a bewildering array of committees. Do we over complicate and create too many committees? Boards would do well to ask this question as part of their annual review process. On the one hand, there's a lot to deal with. On the other, duplication can occur and those who sit on these committees are volunteering their precious time.

Recruitment to safeguarding and special educational needs and disabilities (SEND) governors is proving increasingly difficult, unsurprising given the complexity of the subjects and the time required to be a diligent contributor.

*Which of these committees does your board have? Which do you sit on and why? Which gives you a sense of fulfilment? In the spirit of saving governors' time, which would you merge?*

- Audit and risk
- Wellbeing
- Finance
- Safeguarding
- People/HR
- SEND
- Remuneration
- Policy development
- Estate and buildings
- Curriculum and assessment
- Careers and destinations
- Standards and examinations
- Inclusion
- Inspection and review
- Appeals
- Disciplinary

Membership of committees rightly plays to the skills and knowledge of different board members; in any group one quickly acknowledges someone worth listening to keenly. Often governors are reluctant to be moved around to other committees and of course their preferences should be respected. That said, enabling everyone to glimpse how various committees operate offers valuable training opportunities. Furthermore, from time to time, committees may host observers – perhaps thinking about putting themselves forward as a governor/trustee – to hear their rich conversations in action.

Key to the success of committees is the precision with which their terms of reference are drafted and thoughtfully interpreted. A school's or trust's committee structure, when skilfully chaired, conducted and minuted, can make or break the overall wellbeing and effectiveness of the main board.

In turn, excellent *communication* between the main board and the committees – through the respective chairs, notes of meetings, executive 'link' colleagues – is decisive. Where the system falters, where agreeable disagreements break out, invariably communication has been poor. Even amongst willing governors, it can be a cardinal feature of change that someone will (deliberately) misunderstand something they do not quite agree with!

## WHERE DOES THE BUCK STOP?

To return to our French general at the start of the chapter, is it actually the deputy principal who lands the deal, who solves the problems, who leads from behind?

The final responsibility for decision making lies with the paid leaders of the organisation: the CEO, principal, headteacher. Their job descriptions and salaries reflect exactly that. Good chairs will always strive – in tandem with their fellow board members – to ensure that wise decisions have been taken through proper processes, and that those decisions are correctly recorded and carefully communicated. Ultimate *accountability* is with governors.

What usually shines through when sometimes difficult decisions are later reviewed is that the vast majority of volunteer governors practised their governance in good faith, ever with a focus on what is in the best interests of children and young people. They take delegation seriously and reflect keenly when there are lessons to be learned. Open dialogue between those who govern and those who are governed is a prerequisite.

We do not get it right all of the time and proceed humbly in that certainty.

# ASIDE
## WHAT TO DO?

The chair, vice-chair, principal and vice-principal have met to consider applications for the assistant principal post due to be vacated at the end of term. The applications include a number of very promising candidates so a decision is made to call them for interview.

However, budget uncertainties dominate further conversations.

- Is it better to fill the gap by some restructuring of the senior team? Issue: additional pressures on senior team.
- Is it better to wait until next term when finances may be clearer? Issue: losing some good candidates.

*The answer to the questions needs to come from the governors. . .*

\*\*\*\*

There is a proposal to set up a new sports academy in the sixth form, subject to governor ratification. This involves entering into a formal arrangement with a local sports club. This club has an existing working relationship with the school, and there is potential for wider working, including supporting students beyond sport, and for extending this to key stage 4.

Some vocal governors are asking for assurance that this proposal aligns to the school's vision, and for clarity of lines of responsibility including on communications and marketing.

Furthermore, what is the proposed governance model? How will governors make sure that the arrangement is working? How will they manage any adverse publicity surrounding the sports club, which might impact on the school? Who will manage that in a worst-case scenario? How will governors manage safeguarding?

*What do governors decide?. . .*

\*\*\*\*

# EXECUTIVE

**Knowing where governance ends, and executive practice begins, is a hallmark of the successful board.**

Forged out of revolution and separation from a 'homeland', the American constitution created three branches of government: the executive, the legislative and the judicial. Successive US presidents have flexed their executive powers to test the relative powers of Congress and the Supreme Court. In our time, President Trump has put on a headline-grabbing display.

At the heart of effective governance in schools and trusts is an open and transparent appreciation by all parties as to what the executive's responsibilities and limits of power are, and the complementary responsibilities of governors and trustees. Get that right as a team, and the organisation will flourish; get that wrong and undue delay, worry, pain, even chaos, can ensue.

## WHAT IS OPERATIONAL?

Hospitals, airports and schools are often compared in the media and in political circles for relative busyness and complexity. The latter is not open for 24 hours a day, 7 days a week, 365 days of the year – so probably comes third in the list. Yet spend a day – from 7am opening to 9pm closing – in a school and you realise just how many human interactions are compressed into those hours.

Take an average size secondary school.

The site manager and his team open up and clean from 7am; 100 teaching and support staff arrive from 7.30am, meet, greet and start their planning; 1000 young people start to drift in from when the library opens at 7.45am; 8.30am and the first of what will be 1000+ lessons begins, with all the richness they deliver. Breaktimes, lunchtimes, after-school clubs and meetings, bus departures, more cleaning – then adult education and sports clubs for the local community start. The deputy site manager jingles his keys, sets the alarms and leaves late at 9.30pm.

All that energetic complexity is *operational* and is self-evidently the province of the school's executive to oversee. The triumphs and disasters of the day belong to the staff and students – and for 190 days a year that's how it goes.

Governors may well be in school in one capacity or another during a regular school week, engaging with leaders, teachers and students; they fully understand they are not operational. They may comment later at a board meeting on something they enjoyed or have questions about. Good governance knows its boundaries, and robust protocols about board members visiting schools are generally well respected. Exceptions arise and are promptly sorted. Very exceptional cases occur – and waste everyone's time.

*To intervene or not as a governor?*

- You see Year 11 students on their phones at breaktime in a school that bans phones.
- You watch two members of staff walking through the corridor with open coffee cups, ignoring disorderly behaviour.
- You hear a group of Year 8s using offensive language.

Such scenarios are useful to rehearse because they test the line between strategic and operational, albeit on what might be perceived as minor matters. With respect to agreed protocols, common sense amongst adults should prevail.

## WHAT IS STRATEGIC?

To make a link with the three scenarios above:

- Governors will certainly have rehearsed the ever-topical issue of mobile phones; the decision reached (not necessarily unanimously) will be implemented by the staff.

- Governors will certainly have discussed, agreed and signed off health and safety regulations – staff carrying open coffee cups are in breach.
- Governors will have debated and agreed a behaviour and attitudes policy; those Year 8s are sadly offending.

When governors visit schools, especially those who know the local community well, they often see incidents that are on the edge of rule-breaking, which they also see in that local community. For them sometimes it is not easy to stand back and not intervene, even if they do it with a twinkle in their eye. The executive and governors would do well to discuss these matters openly in everyone's best interests.

As in many aspects of running schools, some things are black and white, like evacuation procedures, whilst others can be grey in interpretation. Living with the grey and interpreting it thoughtfully and creatively marks out wise governance and effective relationships between the board and school leaders.

Stepping back from the everyday commerce of corridors and classrooms, it is usually the case that board and committee meetings of schools and trusts are dominated by strategic matters, major and minor.

In a school it may be about admissions limits, building expansions, staffing levels, curriculum changes – issues which often will have been first discussed in committees and are now with the main board for decisions.

In a trust context, on a larger scale and with more zeros in the budget, it may be about expanding central staff; or having three new schools join; or how long to keep subsidising one school's falling rolls; or introducing a new reading programme across all schools. Each of these can involve months and months of preparation by leaders, ably supported by teachers and administrators.

Best practice suggests that each major topic would have been discussed by the board and its committees at regular intervals and to an agreed timeline, with transparent documentation. Due diligence processes may well have been implemented. Thus, when a final board decision is taken, all trustees feel they have had ample opportunity to shape these significant next steps – and are content to affirm that they advance.

## HOW ARE LINES DRAWN IN PRACTICE?

Experience indicates that in most contexts, most of the time, school and trust leaders have established excellent working relationships with the governing board and trust one another to exercise common sense interpretations of what is strategic and what is operational. That way, the organisation flourishes day by day, term by term and over the years. Best practice will include all members of the senior leadership team. A reminder that it is wise not to rely totally on the head or principal – they will occasionally be away – and this provides excellent professional development.

(Of note here is that when deputy heads are being interviewed for headship, when asked the question about their relative knowledge gaps, they frequently cite lack of experience working with governors.)

It does not hurt to reflect carefully on those occasions when, for one reason or another, there has been disquiet about how the strategic and the operational have been interpreted to the point where there have been prickly exchanges. Timing and communication – mistiming and miscommunication – usually lie at the heart of prickly exchanges, personalities aside!

Reflective governors will have also decided with the executive team whether there are particular matters that are best left to each other, with communication lines kept properly open. Does the chair involve themselves with professional associations? Does the principal involve themselves with district councillors? And who restrains whom when it comes to lively exchanges with parents about changing the school hours?!

A note here also about how long a chair has been in post, how long the governing body have been together, how new or well established is the executive – each of these shapes ways of doing and working relationships. Where kindness and mutual respect are watchwords, governance flourishes. Trust takes time to build. A successful modus operandi is not born overnight.

## FRANKLY SPEAKING

Interview a number of experienced chairs and school/trust leaders on the subject of what is important in their ways of working with one another, and three regularly shared themes emerge.

*Frankness*: 'We know we'll speak our minds to one another in private – and it's important we do that on a regular basis.'

*Surprises*: 'I do not want to get to a meeting and it's the first time I've heard of something.'

*Collusion*: 'It's important that we work well together but not to the point where others think we are colluding and taking all the decisions.'

These offer a fair recipe to getting things right between the governed and those who govern.

---

# ASIDE

## WHAT TO DO?

An opportunity arises to create a second SEND resource base in this maintained school. The local authority needs to secure additional SEND provision in local secondary schools. The headteacher has given a 'positive in principle' message to governors, combined with some real anxieties about how it will work.

Pressure on the school's current SEND provision is growing, although the track record is strong. Most governors want to be helpful to the local authority. The chair of finance and audit wants to see a concrete proposition that addresses the opportunities and all the key risks/mitigations. In particular:

- Are the capital works manageable on the timescale proposed?
- Are the numbers of students and their needs categories acceptable to the school, and what are the admissions procedures?
- Is the funding and the support for recruitment sufficient?
- Is the position of the current resource base protected?

---

*Next steps from the board?...*

\*\*\*\*

A member of the board is being approached by parents within the community to raise personal issues relating to their children's experience at school. What started as a one-off incident is becoming a bit of a habit, which is beginning to have an impact on the running of board meetings — e.g. straying from the agenda — and is encouraging a culture of lobbying within the community.

*How do governors address this?...*

AND

A newly appointed member of the board is keen to draw upon their business experience and get involved in the day-to-day running of the school to help with streamlining operations. This is having an impact on the running of board meetings — e.g. getting bogged down in minutiae — and crossing the line between governance and leadership, and management.

*What action is required here?...*

\*\*\*\*

# **F** FIRES

**Addressing and resolving conflicts and emergencies are true tests of confident governance.**

A long-serving local education authority chief officer used to tell a delightful tale about possessive headteachers and why they should never use the phrase 'my school'. One such headteacher spoke at every meeting of 'my school, my school' in such a way that it came across that she was the only person that mattered in the school community.

One day, a major fire broke out at the school. The head at once called the chief officer and exclaimed: *'Our* school is burning, can you help quickly please?'

Arguably, governance in tandem with the executive is all about putting out proverbial fires before they even start, certainly heading off emerging crises and, in a 24-hour media age, anticipating if anything threatens the wellbeing and good reputation of the institution.

## STARTING WITHIN

Experienced chairs know this – but it never hurts to do a revision course. If you are a chair new to role, the executive leader (probably accompanied by the clerk) will run you through just how the organisation as a whole operates. As you are doing this, keep a notebook handy and jot down anything that occurs to you that just might, just might, lead to a metaphorical fire. As a chair probably with experience in other workplaces, it is important to bring what you know from other contexts. Do not assume, do not presume. Educationalists do not have all the answers.

The wisdom of hindsight is a wonderful human trait; confident governance is all about *anticipation* – and while it would be super-human to know what lies on the horizon – and events intervene – it is perfectly possible to be thoughtfully prepared.

For example, have governors rehearsed with the executive what action would be taken in the following scenarios?

- You are subject to a ransomware attack.
- A violent intruder is spotted in the school grounds.
- There are suddenly two cases of meningitis in the sixth form.
- The school receives an anonymous phone call saying that school meals today have been spiked.
- Heavy snow falls during the morning, and a third of your students come by bus from neighbouring villages.
- A fifth of the staff who belong to a particular professional association say they are joining an unofficial two-day regional strike.

****

Talk to any headteacher and they will say that the event that you cannot prepare for personally is the death of a child or adult in the school community. In my experience that is true. Of course, there will be clearly drafted guidelines to follow in the event of such a tragedy. It is worth thinking and talking through – perhaps with a small group of governors – how the board should support staff, students and families in the event of a major incident.

Clearly set out and rehearsed guidelines exist in every institution for such things as fire evacuation, lockdown and violent incidents; it is valuable to satisfy yourselves as a board in advance of any of these happening just what is expected of all stakeholders. Getting it wrong will first and foremost have a profound effect on any victims. Second, getting it wrong will reverberate through the organisation for months afterwards, potentially weighing very heavily on leaders at all levels.

In a 24/7 social media age, decisive action and *rapid transparency* are the watchwords. There are not many principals and governing bodies today who do not have scripted press releases, emails and letters to families ready to go in the event of a major incident.

## STUDENTS AND STAFF

When there are breaches of behaviour codes by students or staff, schools and trusts are usually well prepared with relevant documentation that outlines clearly what steps need taking – in the interests of those who have allegedly breached rules and the rest of the school community.

Governors may well be involved in subsequent disciplinary and exclusion panels. A wise board has thought through meticulously which governors are unconflicted and so can sit on panels, and which governors are kept in reserve for appeal. The chair and the principal will lead on this, frequently supported by HR colleagues from within the trust or within the local authority. In a litigious age, sadly, families threatening trusts and school with lawyers is sometimes never far behind and invariably takes up a disproportionate amount of leadership time.

School leaders know that handling disciplinary breaches and follow-up actions are part of the job – 'twas ever thus and forever will be.

What is increasingly the case however is the involvement of the so-called 'keyboard warriors' in the online community, aggravating incidents and seeking to unsettle professional leaders. Experienced governors can play a significant role here in being a sounding board for principals and, yes, pushing back on attempts to worsen a situation through exaggeration or misinformation. Talking this through at a people committee one afternoon would be time well spent.

## LOOKING OUTWARDS

When a trust or school looks outwards, scans the educational horizon, what challenges is it anticipating? There will be a local, regional and national dimension to this, from Newcastle to Plymouth, from Dover to Preston. It is time well invested for a small group of interested governors – working with the executive – to brainstorm what they see. Budgets and buildings always feature, with teacher recruitment and, in some contexts, falling rolls.

Anticipating the highs and lows – especially the lows – helps prepare an organisation for any serious jolts to its day-to-day running. In the commercial world, the financial bottom-line looms ever large. Arguably, that same financial preoccupation is increasingly part of the education landscape.

Contemporary debate around working from home and the four-day week is a topic of discussion in many boards, allied to the recruitment and retention of teaching and support staff. What thoughts on these subjects is your board shaping?

## BOARD FIRES

The trusted and open relationship between the chair and the executive leader, which lies at the core of successful governance, can be tested from time to time, deliberately or inadvertently. That relationship always makes sure that it is never one of collusion, or indeed perceived collusion, such that other governors can come to feel resentful that in the end their voice does not matter – 'it's just the chair who counts'.

Yet fires can break out within the board on matters of principle, on matters of local planning, on matters of school policy and their implementation, on matters of donations – large and small – from sources some members do not agree with.

At times, there is a slow burn of a difference of opinion emanating from a committee discussion. The balance a chair needs to strike is to ensure that the whole board listens when a strong voice wants to air their views, whilst at the same time reminding members that the need to 'unite all differences intact' is in the end what will best serve the children and young people. Trustees and governors are voices, they are not representatives.

Rarely, resignations on matters of principle occur. They should be accepted in good spirit, with an individual's position respected; that person leaves with dignity. The mature board notes the departure and writes a letter of sincere thanks for their service. We remind ourselves again that we are here as volunteers, not subject to employment law.

## AFTERMATH

Records over the past 50 years across the nation's schools happily show just a few cases of arson and otherwise minor interruptions to the school day from fires. The unearthing in recent years of RAAC (reinforced autoclaved aerated concrete) in a number of schools has proved far more disruptive; and the dreaded asbestos has a habit of erupting any time.

Yet the proverbial fires – disciplinary matters, professional disputes, resignations – can seriously shake a school, and they can come out of nowhere, suddenly on the front page of a local newspaper. It is not possible to anticipate and prevent troubling events. It is possible to be as best prepared as a board can be.

Furthermore, the dust eventually settles. What is then important is that any damaged relationships are repaired, and the organisation moves on, genuinely telling itself that it is stronger for having been tested.

Teachers and parents are sometimes quick to lament the lack of resilience of today's young people. Leaders and governors need to model strong reliance and optimism in the aftermath of an event that has temporarily rocked the school community. Live to thrive for another day – and read Dylan Thomas's delightful *A Child's Christmas in Wales* (Thomas, 1954): '"Call the fire brigade … Let's call the police as well," Jim said. "And the ambulance. And Ernie Jenkins, he likes fires."'

# ASIDE

## WHAT TO DO?

A new headteacher appointment is to be made at the local primary school. The school has been led very successfully for a decade, so there is nervousness amongst families and governors about securing the new headteacher.

A couple of well-meaning parent governors circulate on social media a questionnaire, which asks what qualities are expected in the new headteacher. Predictably, the returns pose as many questions as answers.

The parent governors table a summary of findings at a board meeting, and expect to be on the interviewing panel. Other governors push back and seek a postponement to any interview process.

*What next?...*

**** 

The rise of the need for panels of governors to hear complaints and staff and student disciplinary cases, and attend meetings and visit the school is causing challenges for the board. Staff governors cannot get involved and not all parents are able to.

This often leaves some retired board members as panel attendees, which is leading some to consider whether they want that level of responsibility and time commitment in a volunteer position. And recruiting governors of high quality is not getting any easier.

The headteacher is bound to act in line with the policies and wants to explore how the board could manage this differently.

*The board meets with this topic as a major item...*

****

# GUESTS

**Thoughtful boards know when to look outwards to refresh their established thinking and practices.**

Can any bus service rival the fine Hanley to Bagnall route in Staffordshire? It was reported that the buses no longer stopped for passengers. This came to light when one of them, Mr Bill Hancock, complained that buses on the outward journey regularly sailed past queues of up to 30 people.

The archives of the county council record that Councillor Arthur Cholerton made transport history by stating that if these buses stopped to pick up passengers they would disrupt the timetable.

Good governance welcomes planned 'disruption' and 'disruptors' – even and especially when their organisation is flourishing – in the shape of invited guests. Experienced boards always make clear to invitees what the rules of engagement are and the purpose of their joining meetings.

Some governing bodies and many trust boards routinely have short pre-meetings without executive members present; these can be important to give a fair airing to a subject that trustees feel needs study without executive members present. If handled well by the chair and the CEO, this does not lead to any sense of 'us and them', rather to a mutual respect that we all have different roles in wise governance.

## INSIDERS

In this category it is right to include the senior leadership team (SLT); they are indeed guests of the governors or trustees. Very often one member of the SLT will work very closely with one of the governors, say on finance, and effective common practice is that executive members pair up with governors who chair committees. These relationships and mutual understanding are vital to successful governance.

It is imperative that senior leaders 'speak less and listen more' at board meetings, probably having had more to say at committees. One board has a rule of thumb that the executive should not speak for more than a total of 10 minutes in 60, allowing trustees space to think and debate. Try a stopwatch at your next governors' meeting!

Board meetings are frequently enriched by teachers and students being invited to present a particular topic to develop everyone's understanding before decisions are made. For example, the school wishes the board to approve a major investment in a new whole-school reading scheme; the language coordinator arrives to explain its merits and share some sample materials. Or the board are being asked to make a new appointment in the creative arts arena; a couple of teachers from that curriculum area come to explain what the impact on students will be from a new post.

Students too make welcome guests. The board may be discussing the need for enhanced Year 11 study facilities; three students are asked to say why and how they would design such facilities. There are plans to make an investment in the playing fields; four students with a deep commitment to sport are invited to give their views.

Opening up board meetings – keeping to time – is invariably positive for staff and student personal development, positive for building trust, and positive for governors to hear first-hand information before taking careful decisions for the school community.

## OUTSIDERS

In the multi-academy trust world, members of the central trust team would probably call themselves 'insiders'. Suffice to say they are an integral part of the team, whether holding headteachers to account for academic standards and balancing their budgets or working alongside leaders on estate management and personnel issues. The best trusts certainly have established excellent working relationships, clarity of roles and a 'mutual holding to account' between principals and central staff.

Local authority schools will have similar good relationships with local education advisers, HR and campus management staff, and very often with those outstanding directors of education who make it their business to be in primary, special and secondary schools as often as they can. When these same directors then speak about special educational needs funding to political members, they are known to do so from first-hand experience. This is greatly valued by school leaders and their governing bodies.

Parent governors are elected in the knowledge that they are not representatives of other parents; they are there with their own voices, in their own right.

Rightly they bring the crucial parent perspective to a discussion on changing the times of the school day or changes to school uniform. On such topics, boards or committees may choose to invite three or four parents of different aged students to a meeting so that their views are canvassed, which is important in ensuring trust between boards and families. Boards of course must be prepared to take a decision that they consider serves the majority, rather than sometimes a vocal minority; or they have very good reasons to follow that minority view.

## HOW ARE GOVERNORS PERCEIVED BY STAFF?

Let's turn the mirror the other way round.

In staff meetings, headteachers often refer to governors' meetings, without always making explicit who the governors are, and indeed how they are an integral part of leadership. Governors can remain a mystery, certainly to much of the staffroom who probably only know the staff governors well.

*What do teachers' voices record about their perceptions of governors? Here's a sample:*

'To me they were distant figures with splendid white hair, glimpsed going into the head's office for important meetings or listened to keenly on annual speech days.'

'Would be good to know who they are: their names and photos on the staffroom board.'

'Transparency of purpose – what do governors actually do? Certainly wouldn't be clear to many of my colleagues if asked…'

'Smile! Governors have this slightly other-worldly aura when viewed from the classroom – when they are spoken of (admittedly not often), it is in hushed tones of slightly awed reverence. I've encountered governors who seem to revel in this impression, and while I'm sure some degree of separation between governors and teachers is advisable, it strikes me that it wouldn't go amiss for certain governors to be reminded that they are on the same team as the teachers, all rowing in the same direction… (I've also met governors who do, yes, smile, and it makes a massive difference.)'

'The only time most teachers will encounter the chair of governors (certainly in my limited experience) is in a start of year/term whole-staff briefing, so these small snapshots matter! It will often be the only impression lots of staff get of the governors (represented by proxy by the chair) for several months or even a whole year, so putting some thought into the words and tone of any message to all staff is very important.'

'It's nice to be recognised by the governors. When we have had some collective successes as a school recently, the chair has sent a message round to all staff, which has been appreciated.'

'Could they say something interesting about the role of staff governors? I know lots of staff are put off applying for the post due to rumoured length (and lateness) of meetings.'

'Their presence at school events is noted (if pointed out…) and valued – school concerts, careers fairs, plays, PTA events, etc.'

## SUGGESTED ACTION

Holding up the mirror is as good a way as any to gain 360-degree feedback.

Many schools have a governors' noticeboard in their staffrooms, and in addition to a copy of the latest minutes, this includes a list of governors with photos and the committees they sit on. The safeguarding and SEND governors may well be better known to certain teachers and support staff.

Board chairs/headteachers might agree to send a joint, short email summary of key points covered and key decisions made within a couple of days of each meeting.

Boards should agree to make sure that whenever members are in school, they work to certain protocols (see page 143) – and smile in the right places!

---

# ASIDE

## WHAT TO DO?

A newly appointed parent governor has a child with a range of additional needs. The new governor has become a very vocal and dominant voice at meetings and always about issues affecting his child. Other governors have expressed their concern to the headteacher and chair about this.

The new governor has attended training yet feels his mandate as the elected member for parents vindicates his approach. The headteacher has said clearly to the chair that this new governor is not being managed properly.

The board have this question of parents 'representing other parents' as a matter for discussion at the next board meeting.

*What arguments unfold?. . .*

\*\*\*\*

---

One member of the board does not see the value in the school being part of the multi-academy trust it is in, and has been forceful in suggesting the school is brokered to another trust, which he has confidence in.

He has also been the one governor on the board to submit expenses for his time — and has been encouraging others to do the same 'because that's what this other trust provides for governors'.

The board have become dominated by discussions on whether to change trusts, at the expense of matters relating to the strategic direction of the school and its current priorities. The chair is increasingly unsure how to manage this.

A meeting is arranged with this topic as a single item.

*What results?...*

****

# HOUSEKEEPING

## The wise governing body has shared expectations of its own housekeeping rules.

In Charles Dickens's 1850 novel *David Copperfield*, the legendary character Mr Micawber warns eloquently about debt: 'Annual income twenty pounds, annual expenditure nineteen nineteen and six, result happiness. Annual income twenty pounds, annual expenditure twenty pound ought and six, result misery' (Dickens, 1850).

A governing body's firm grasp of finance is one pivotal aspect of their work. Looking after their own wider domestic affairs lays the groundwork for effective governance. And these aspects are not to be underestimated for a group of volunteers coming together from time to time. The domestics and hygiene factors play a well-researched part in whether volunteers turn up for meetings regularly, and how long they stay on boards.

## TIME AND TIMINGS

### The meeting cycle

'It's not what is in the diary that kills you. It's what is not in the diary.'

The ancient Greeks had two understandings of time, *chronos* and *kairos*. Both are important, but the latter rarely gets the attention it warrants. It deserves to.

*Chronos* time is chronological time: how we measure our days and our lives quantitatively. We have been setting our lives by some form of chronological time for centuries, judging by our cultural lexicon – 'time waits for no one', 'time is of the essence', 'time is money'.

Perhaps we should also look at things through the prism of *kairos*. How do we honour *kairos* time, what the ancient Greeks understood as the most opportune time for something new? The concept has its origins in the practice of Greek archery, representing the moment when the archer finds the perfect opening to shoot their arrow and hit the target. Kairos was also the Greek god of opportunity. He had wings on his feet and darted quickly about.

So in establishing a meeting cycle it is critical that it is set in a way which best enables governors to come together when school leaders judge meetings are timely. Too often there can be rather lazy calendaring of meetings 'because we have always done it this way'. Strong boards will challenge those orthodoxies and think through carefully with the executive whether, for example, October rather than September or May rather than June are better fits. Think *kairos* as much as *chronos,* as much as financial year ends.

Governors are volunteers so their availability within their own busy personal and professional lives is a key factor. The thoughtful clerk will sound out when governors are unlikely to be around. Once done, it is generally advisable to set a meeting schedule in July for a school year ahead, and make this available promptly to governors with all term and half-term dates, training days, etc.

The meeting cycle is further complicated by the best timing – and how often – for committees to meet in relation to the main board. Again, governors should not be afraid to challenge entrenched ways of doing, though sometimes those well-established patterns work well, so there is no need for change, just modest adaptation. There are rules about meetings being quorate; the clerk will advise.

## Times of day

Many school leaders have tales to tell about watching their lives slip away as the governors' meeting, which started at 7pm, finally arrived at any other business (AOB) at 9.55pm. Are those days largely gone? We all hope so in an age of respecting volunteers' time and the workload of school leaders. That said, if refreshments at 6pm and a well conducted meeting 6.30pm – 8pm works for the participants, then timetable it.

There are rarely times of the day to suit all stakeholders, and it's usually a careful balancing act – and trial and error if it is early days for a new board, or an established board welcoming a few new members. With flexible work habits more of a feature in society than was hitherto the case, many governing boards and committees choose to meet from 2pm, allowing pupils and staff to be involved in proceedings without calling them back after school. Cover arrangements for some schools mean headteachers prefer a 4pm start.

Many trust boards opt for a whole morning, or whole afternoon, complete with pre-meetings, refreshments and some social time with the executive. That may also include visiting auditors or other external voices. And timely refreshments, water on the table, cold drinks on hot days, hot drinks on cold days – never forget!

What of the optimum meeting length? One hour for a committee, short and focused? Two hours maximum for the board, three hours with a good break? Trial and test, and err on the side of brevity – allow no more than five slides for a presentation at any meeting.

## VENUES

What kind of meeting room do you enjoy being in, for several hours? Executive leaders need to give this question the attention it deserves. We all have stories of our own about meeting in cold halls, sitting on furniture not fit-for-purpose and with lighting making it hard to read important papers. To this day one hears of governors being squashed together around tables without suitable space, light or warmth.

Spaces for meetings in schools vary enormously, from having to meet in the head's office in a small primary to quite palatial conference suites in large secondary schools. The wise governing body needs to be selfish and say that to do its job well the conditions for committees and main board meetings must be conducive to good decision making.

It is often the case too that the rooms governors meet in are given over to inspectors when they call. Look around the room. What are the walls projecting about the values, visions and high expectations of the school? Shouldn't we as governors be surrounded by powerful images and words that inspire us when we meet, and inspire us further to afford the insights and oversight expected of us?

Furthermore, never underestimate the power of furniture configuration. How are tables and chairs set out – in square, circles, ovals? Experience and research tell us that seating arrangements have a measurable impact on the quality of commerce and talk through a meeting. Can the chair see the whites of everyone's eyes? Can board members see the whites of the chair's eyes? Can we see the projected slides clearly; can we read the tiny data flashed in front of us on a screen?

A famous politician once observed that the mind can assimilate only as much as the behind can tolerate. He went on to say that 'speeches should only be given on a full bladder' to prevent politicians going on for too long. In the course of every meeting, half an eye on the clock, the chair should not hesitate to call for a strict ten-minute toilet and refreshments break as required: minds and bladders can be cleared. Anyone who has managed a tricky meeting knows intuitively when to call a comfort break.

****

A board's own housekeeping arrangements are too important to be left to chance. Too often there is a casual acceptance of 'this is how and when and where we meet, and this is how things are'.

Chairs, sometimes having to challenge the executive, need to satisfy themselves that arrangements for meetings are the best they can be, given finite resources. Fine decision making hinges upon how governors are *feeling* as well as thinking.

The CEO of one of the major tourist hotspots in the UK testifies to the fact that all the feedback he receives is *not* about the quality of the attractions. It *is* about parking, toilets, refreshments – in that order. Trust boards make a point of holding some meetings in their schools as well as trust offices; ease and difficultly of travel must be factored in too for everyone involved. Maximising attendance at every meeting is the careful goal for which there is collective responsibility.

# ASIDE

## WHAT TO DO?

The trust board have agreed to do a self-assessment of their strengths and areas for development as individuals, beyond a standard skills mapping audit.

Although some of the trust schools are underperforming, the results of the survey are exceptionally positive, with no trustees identifying any weaknesses.

The trust chair is acutely aware how much everyone already generously gives of their time, and is anxious not to lose people, but disagrees with their collective self-analysis. She decides to tackle this head-on at the next trust board meeting.

*How does she go about this?. . .*

\*\*\*\*

A new parent governor is increasingly using formal governing body meetings to generalise about a school's possible failings based on the experiences of their best friend, whose child also attends the school.

The parent governor has said they will try to contact as many other parents whom they know, in order to confirm their hypotheses. They want to share their research at the next meeting.

*How does the governing body respond?. . .*

\*\*\*\*

# INTERVIEWS

**Staging and managing high quality interviews of all descriptions are at the core of strong governance.**

One of the more memorable interviews I was ever party to involved Sister Marie.

I had been asked by a diocesan leader to join interviews for the headship of a school. The powerful chair, Father McMadden, welcomed three regular governors, the county's primary adviser and me. We interviewed five candidates over two hours in the presbytery.

In his brief summing up, the chair announced that Sister Marie would be appointed. We had not interviewed her. She had not been one of the candidates. The primary adviser advised – I duly nodded – that it was irregular to appoint a candidate we had not met. Father left the room, made a telephone call, returned and asked us to have a cup of tea while Sister Marie drove across the city to meet us.

Sister duly arrived, sat down at the table for all of 15 minutes, was asked a small number of questions and then left. In his second summing up, the chair announced Sister Marie's appointment, unanimously agreed.

****

That was then. And whether we are an education leader or a leader in any other walk of life, we each have our own tales to tell of successful and unsuccessful interviews, of left-field questions, of mistakes we made, of answers we gave that were really good ones, of idiosyncratic interviewers with whom we did not get on.

It remains the case that conducting high quality interviews, to agreed protocols, is a central and enjoyable responsibility of governors and trustees. During a typical period of office, governors will be asked to take part in a range of interviews, usually for senior posts within schools and the trust.

## PREPARATION

Experience suggests that today's interviews in the education workplace are characterised by a highly professional approach, from first advertisement to a candidate signing the contract. That said, governors frequently bring fresh eyes to tried and tested educational processes, and, if invited to participate, should not be shy in asking for the whole process to be explained. And why do you do it this way?

The executive will usually have identified the need to fill a particular post and will draft an appropriate job description. To agreed procedures within the school or trust, the post will be advertised openly and transparently. There are occasions when the post may be advertised internally only, mindful of requirements within employment law. References will doubtless be followed through within an established framework.

As a governor invited to be involved, ask for clarity about your role. Are you to take part in shortlisting as well as interviewing? What is the time commitment and the timescale? Are you available on the interview day(s)?

Watch any craftsperson at work, and the success of the final outcome lies in the preparation. Much the same applies with successful recruitment: attention to detail matters at every stage so that once the process is complete everyone involved – interviewers and interviewees – feels the right outcome has been properly achieved.

## INTERVIEWS

Interviews for senior posts usually involve a timetable of activities in a school or in trust offices, meeting various stakeholders and undertaking a range of oral and written tasks. These will be skilfully orchestrated by the executive. Governors may well be asked to meet each candidate for half an hour and discuss a particular topic, and governors should have an input into what that topic might be. Each governor will have their own ideas; these might be starters:

*What kinds of open questions elicit the person as well as the professional?*

- What books and thinkers about education and working with children have influenced you over the years?
- Would you recommend just one book that everyone you are working with should read, to get a sense of who you are as a leader?
- What do you see as the great opportunities with this role?
- From looking around the school and talking to staff and students, are there a couple of obstacles that will be important to tackle in your first hundred days?
- What kind of pace of change and development does this organisation need now?

There may be a plan to sift say five candidates on the day to two or three for final interviews. Experiences suggest that leaders handle feedback/feedforward very well to unsuccessful candidates, and as a governor your reflections will be valued.

It is at a final interview that governors very often come into their own. They bring wise experiences from other contexts and can think through objectively which candidate is the best fit. Sometimes executive members will openly say that they feel too close to a given context and especially value that more distant view from a governor or trustee.

In coming to a conclusion, best practice enables the chair of the interviewing panel to ask each member to offer their thoughts, usually rooted in some kind of scoring template of common questions to candidates. Best practice avoids voting; rather, a well-argued consensus is reached.

Effective practice will also include a short wrap-up with the interviewing board: what did we do well as interviewers? How might we do better next time? The chair of governors Robert Palmer, referenced on page 5, used to say that if we interviewed five candidates, we should remember that the panel was warming up with the first one and was tired when the last one came into the room – our conclusions had to be thus tempered. He was always worth listening to.

The overall process is a serious one, but should not be solemn. After all, we are talking about the joys of teaching and learning with young people. Feedback from successful and unsuccessful candidates will comment that the process has been an enjoyable and fair one if positive relationships, humour, seriousness, clarity and precision have underpinned the day.

## APPOINTMENT OF CEO OR HEADTEACHER

Experienced governors know that there will be no more important task during their tenure than the appointment of a headteacher, a principal, a CEO. This is a particularly high stakes point in time for an organisation of any size and scale.

All of the above procedures will apply, possibly with the addition of an external recruitment agency talking to a group of governors delegated by the board to see through the appointment.

Experiences across the system indicate that governors and trustees take this opportunity to seriously review the current successes, challenges and opportunities ahead for their organisation and its context:

- Do we need new leadership that sustains what we have, with modest change?
- Do we want to appoint someone who will bring greater urgency to our school development plan?
- Are we at a point in time when we need to take more measured risks?

What is particular about these questions is that governors, as guardians of the values and vision of the school or trust, are especially well placed to rehearse these questions to help them shape this vital appointment. And, as ever with appointments, you need just one excellent candidate who, at the end of a rigorous interview process, needs to feel 'this is the job for me'.

## POSTSCRIPT

In my experience of countless hours of interviews, one of the unintended outcomes has been that the time governors spend together on panels and through interview days leads to them knowing one another as people so much better than they did just through board and committee meetings.

This is not a recipe for an organisation to create staff churn in order to involve governors in more interviews. Yet it is a reminder that the volunteer governor has a wealth of individual personal experiences to bring to the table – and when they interweave with their fellow governors' substantial knowledge and skills, the combination is rich. Schools and trusts should treasure what their volunteers can add.

# ASIDE

## WHAT TO DO?

The governing body of a previously stand-alone school has recently joined a trust. However, they are putting pressure on the headteacher for their agreement on a range of decisions, which in fact, under the scheme of delegation, sit with the trust board rather than the local governing body.

The chair of the local governing body has contacted the chair of the trust to intervene.

AND

The headteachers of some of the schools within a trust have told the CEO that their local boards feel 'out of the loop' and their opinions and ideas are not heard. The CEO shares this feedback with the trust board, although some trustees feel strongly that there are already mitigating systems in place.

*What conversations ensue at trust board level?. . .*

\*\*\*\*

The chair of governors is long serving on the board and her own children, who are now adults, all went through the school successfully and have fond memories of their time there. The chair of governors has huge respect for the headteacher, who she describes as being inspirational and at the heart of the whole community.

The headteacher has many fine qualities but the governing body has not recognised a decline in pupil outcomes over time. Governors are diligent in reading the headteachers' reports, yet minutes of governor meetings show that there is very little challenge or questioning being presented.

Governors explain that they know their school very well through visiting assemblies, school fêtes and talking to parents in the community. All governors report that from the evidence they see and hear, the students are happy, feel safe and enjoy school.

The school improvement partner's two most recent visits present a very different view of the school.

*What happens next?. . .*

****

# JUDGEMENTS

## The wisdom, timing and communication of decision making shapes top governance.

*The Children Act* (McEwan, 2014) is a novel that should be read by anyone working with children and young people. No spoilers: at the heart of the narrative is a decision a judge must come to about whether to terminate a boy's life.

With characteristic objectivity, sensitivity and precision the judge weighs up what it is to be human. Here is what she says:

> *She listed some relevant ingredients, goals towards which a child might grow. Economic and moral freedom, virtue, compassion and altruism, satisfying work through engagement with demanding tasks, a flourishing network of personal relationships, earning the esteem of others, pursuing larger meanings to one's existence, and having at the centre of one's life one or a small number of significant relations defined above all by love.*

As a reader, it is a passage that stops you in your tracks. As an education leader or as a governor of a school or trust it is well worth a re-read… and a moment of reflection. If we are in the business of educating young lives and shaping their wellbeing and academic successes, does all that we do in our schools hold in mind these 'goals towards which a child might grow'?

Where school leaders and governors share a common loadstar, where there is an excellent shared understanding of the aims and goals of the organisation, that way lies top decision making. In practice, what is the magic cocktail of shaping fine decisions and reliable judgements?

## DECISIONS

Let's take a few practical scenarios:

1. The governing board of a two-form entry primary is asked to consider a local authority request to take a 'bulge entry' of an additional 30 students into the new Year 3, reflecting local housing growth.

2. The governing board of a 1500+ secondary is being asked by the principal to expand the size of the SLT to reflect the increasing needs of disadvantaged and SEND pupils.

3. The board of a multi-academy trust comprising 30 primary and secondary schools is being asked to establish nursery provision in all its 20 primary schools while currently it only has them in two schools.

4. The board of a trust of 40 schools is being asked to agree to ambitious whole-trust academic targets towards 2030 at 11+ and 16+.

Most governors and trustees will recognise these kinds of major decisions, decisions which bind staff, students and families for the long term – and undoubtedly require astute financial and human resource planning.

If the executive gets the following right – the quality of background research, the way in which comprehensive information is presented, the engagement of relevant stakeholders, and the timeline for discussion and final decisions – then informed and trusted conclusions can be reached. If any part of this comes up short, board members, in particular, will be uneasy and reluctant to support next steps.

Experiences in many contexts points to the following as integral to good decision making.

**Hearts and minds**: if there is change afoot, there is usually nervousness from some quarters. It is vital that information provided – in an accessible format – targets the doubting hearts and minds. Linked to scenario 1 above, how have parents in the current Year 2 been consulted and have the practical implications of moving from a two-form to a three-form year group been explained?

**Timing**: linked to scenario 3 above, what's the proposed timeline for this expansion? Who have we consulted? What's the feedback been? Can the trust manage this ambitious programme with current resources? Then the right timing will be make or break.

**Communication**: linked to scenario 4 above, what do teachers across the trust consider are challenging and plausible academic targets? If the board agrees to these targets, how will this be communicated successfully to students, families and teachers?

**Luck**: often underestimated by leaders, luck always plays a part. When major decisions are communicated, what else is going on in people's lives and in the local media?

Watching people in public life, we all know that a very good decision communicated badly can attract opprobrium, whilst a bad decision communicated effectively can be welcomed. 'The medium is the message' as media theorist Marshall McLuhan famously coined (McLuhan, 1964).

The experienced board will sometimes reach the conclusion that the principal or CEO needs restraining at a particular point in time and on a particular issue. The board counsels delay and a request for further information. Board members are frequently best placed to stand back and judge which new initiatives to back or to reject, or to pause on – and where trusting relationships with the executive are secure, matters move on for consideration on another day.

Rooted in a secure understanding of the organisation, that skilful orchestration of people and events marks out the valued board.

## KEEPING THE TRUST/SCHOOL UNDER REVIEW

Great organisations are rooted in excellence as a habit, where high intention, sincere effort and intelligent execution are hallmarks of day-to-day practice. In education this translates as follows:

**High intention**: leaders and teams at all levels set out high, specific ambitions in their respective domains.

**Sincere effort**: all staff approach their daily and weekly tasks with a sincerity and commitment that is personally and professionally satisfying.

**Intelligent execution**: all staff think intelligently and practically about the best ways to achieve their goals, whether as administrators or teachers maximising students' progress and achievements.

How do governors know that all of the above are translating into desired impact, that value for money is being achieved? They do this in many ways, not least with regular reports and data from leaders. What they also do – in common with all successful businesses – is invite external eyes to look over their practices and make recommendations for even-better-ifs.

Commissioned external reviews can come in many forms, and often governors may suggest to the board a commercial source that is well placed to conduct such a review. Local education authorities, of course, perform this role in maintained schools. In each and every context, the board will want to be clear of the purpose and the areas of focus, and commission expertise accordingly. Given financial and other audits take place annually, what the review *does not* spend time on is essential to decide – and beware 'mission creep'.

*How* a review is led and conducted is as important as *what* is being put under the microscope. Get the wrong team doing it and the objectives become self-defeating. Get the right people leading it and there is much value added to the organisation.

Reviews conducted thoroughly take up everyone's time and it is vital for its success that careful consideration is given to both the time of employees that such a review will consume and to fixing a timeline that best fits the rhythm and commitments of the school and trust year. Equally vital is what is agreed by way of when and how the report is to be received, debated and followed up. The involvement of Members should also be considered in this process.

Board members will have a range of experiences of external reviews in different private, public and not-for-profit settings. One example is given in Section Two, page 177.

# ASIDE

## WHAT TO DO?

Anxiety and misinformation had been forming in relation to planned DfE curriculum changes to relationships and sex education. Schools have been advised to hold parental consultation meetings to discuss the change to allay parents' fears.

Following on from such a meeting, a petition was presented to the governing body, asking governors to block the introduction of such changes. The petition included the views of local faith groups within the community.

*How should the governing body proceed?...*

****

A newly appointed and well-intentioned governor is straying into the operational day-to-day matters of the school. She arrives at school without notice and expects to be seen by the headteacher and to be escorted around the school.

When sensitively challenged by the chair of governors and reminded of her strategic role, the governor believes that the headteacher and chair are in collusion in order to avoid constructive challenge.

The governor is vocal in her views to other members of the governing body and quickly establishes support from some other governors. The situation results in a divided governing body with significant hostility to the headteacher and the chair.

*How can this governing body heal this rift to ensure that common purpose prevails?...*

****

# KNOWLEDGE

**The highly respected governing body comprehensively 'knows its onions'.**

In Alexander Pope's poem *An Essay on Criticism* (Pope, 1711), composed in 1709, he wrote:

A little learning is a dangerous thing;

Drink deep, or taste not the Pierian spring: ...

The spring is a reference to mountains sacred to the muses. The same poem also includes these much-quoted lines:

To err is human; to forgive, divine.

and

Fools rush in where angels fear to tread.

Pope offers a veritable treasure trove of advice for governing boards!

What strikes me, in just about every governance context I know, is just how knowledgeable governors and trustees are about the organisation for which they are responsible. It is rare indeed to witness a governor embodying Pope's warning that 'a little learning is a dangerous thing'.

## KNOWLEDGE ABOUT HOW GOVERNANCE WORKS

The Academy Trust Handbook 2024 (Education and Skills Funding Agency, 2024) is a well-crafted 63-page document, and is complemented in local education authorities by governors' handbooks. They are important reading for school and trust leaders, governors and trustees.

The content pages from the 2024 handbook present these key headings under which governors will find answers to most questions they have:

- Roles and responsibilities
- Main financial requirements
- Internal scrutiny
- Annual accounts and external audit
- Delegated authorities
- The regulator and intervention

Of particular note are the words on p.6…

**'must'** – identifies requirements.

**'should'** – identifies minimum good practice.

…and it is time well spent with a board understanding where these words frequently apply. The clerk will always help address misconceptions.

A reasonable understanding of how governance works, and how fine decisions are made rooted in executive recommendations, is characteristic of the vast majority of boards. There are occasional missteps, unintended consequences, and matters to rescue and amend – but to err is to be human.

## KNOWLEDGE ABOUT ORGANISATION

Competent and confident governance is founded on governors having a sound knowledge of the institution's values and vision, of how the budget works and its bottom line, of the people (students and staff) who turn up every day, of the estate for which they are responsible.

What governors bring to the party, in particular, is their local knowledge, their antennae into the community, so that when potentially problematic decisions need taking that will affect families, they are well placed to weigh the pros and cons in a debate and to communicate the outcomes with confidence.

What impresses in so many boards is that members turn up very well prepared, having read papers in advance, often annotating them with questions and points for clarification. Naturally some governors are more interested in finance or buildings or HR, based on their own skill set. Others are fascinated by academic performance data or extra-curricular provision or the latest initiatives with wellbeing. The skilled chair ensures that the sum of the parts is fully harnessed.

## ACCOUNTABILITY MEASURES

In an era of data – sometimes in overwhelming volume – there is no escaping the fact that governors need to be helped to understand educational accountability measures. Principals and headteachers often presume. For them, the acronyms and initialisms of SATs, GCSE, Progress 8, NEETs (Not in Education, Employment or Training) is their professional bread and butter. Chairs of boards often appoint one of their number to nicely 'arrest' the executive every time they employ an acronym that is not commonly understood by the volunteers. It's a worthwhile informal appointment.

Arguably, the devil in the detail is most suitably rehearsed in committees. However, if, for example, a governing body is part of a trust where the seven key performance indicators are all rooted in attainment outcomes over time, then it is behoven on school leaders to explain the data very carefully. Percentages at 'GCSE grade 4 in English and maths combined' may be obvious to the teachers, yet may well need a full explanation to those whose day job is the management of parks or working in social care. They have their own jargon to be sure.

School leaders frequently over-complicate the presentation of data; governors need to push back nicely and ask trenchant questions: what happened last year? What happened this year? Are we seeing reading scores improve or decline? What explains the successes or the shortcomings? Can we have just one page of colour-coded orthographics?

And once you step into the data weeds of SEND, disadvantage, gender or regional variation, these aspects really do need a 'less is more' approach. Over the short, medium and long term, this is time well spent when important decisions are to be made on financing smaller teaching groups or appointing additional teachers. Governors want to feel they are making those investments from a position of fully understanding the context and implications, and the impact on students.

The annual review of examination and test results is an important time for boards and executive to be very transparent with one another in a climate of mutual support and challenge. Anything less and mistrust can set in. The chair and the principal marching in step makes a vital difference here.

## INSPECTION

And, one day, an external inspection arrives. In the spirit of 'no surprises' the wise governing body will be commissioning its own annual reviews from the local authority, an external agency or as an integral part of their being part of a trust.

Through such reviews, the quality of self-evaluation is highlighted. Confident boards know the good, the great and the indifferent about their institution. So, no external visitors can surprise with their commentaries upon students' personal development, the everyday commerce of classrooms, the way leaders get the best out of people and resources, the strengths of inclusion and the curriculum – the smorgasbord that inspectors formally cast their eyes over and make a judgement.

Inspection frameworks come and go; they evolve over time; they embrace fashions and fads of the period; they are politically influenced; they seek to be objective; they are conducted by humans who err and are subjective in their interpretation of criteria. Wise governors accept that and roll with the final report unless they consider that there has been a profound misinterpretation of evidence gathered. There is a clearly stated appeals procedure within every inspection framework.

Furthermore, governors and trustees are optimistic that, in Alexander Pope's words above, inspection teams have 'drunk deep' and captured the heart and spirit of the school community. The published report says much about the school; it is a reflection too on the lead inspector's ability to capture the essence of the rich complexity of school life.

The Ofsted reports featured below, when published, brought real pleasure to pupils, staff and families. The first extract is from a primary school, the second a secondary – what they have in common is their journeys of rapid improvement from low starting points.

## Primary

*Much has changed here in a relatively short period of time. Staff and pupils alike demonstrate boundless energy and great pride in their school. Relationships in classrooms are exceedingly productive. Teachers teach. Pupils learn. There is no time to waste and everyone knows it.*

*Leaders at all levels have a clear vision for the school. This starts at the top with trustees and executive officers from the multi-academy trust. Plans to improve the school are focused. Expectations for success are high. Pupils come first, though the workload and well-being of staff also have an appropriately high priority.*

*Classroom visits show that there is a consistent approach to how the curriculum is delivered across all phases of the school. Staff benefit from a focused and well-planned cycle of internal training. External consultants are also used to enhance the knowledge and expertise of staff. Consequently, pupils experience a high-quality education, no matter what their backgrounds or barriers to learning might be.*

\*\*\*\*

## Secondary

*Pupils rightly recognise how much the school has improved. They explain how the culture has completely changed to one where they are expected to achieve the best they can. The school's values of determination, respect, ambition and kindness are evident in pupils' conduct. Pupils appreciate the higher standards of behaviour across the school. They enjoy learning and work with focus and purpose. This helps them to achieve well. Improvements to the curriculum mean that current pupils are achieving stronger outcomes than previous cohorts.*

*The school promotes a strong and close community. Pupils feel they are known well by their tutors and wider staff. This gives them confidence to share any worries and know they will be supported.*

*They learn about the different cultures in the school through events like 'culture week'. This builds their understanding of others, and pupils view differences as a strength. Around the school, this helps friendships to flourish, regardless of background.*

## FACTS AND FAKE NEWS

An increasing aspect of our social media age is boards having to deal with sometimes hostile press enquiries, sometimes needlessly generated. The received wisdom that these days – that an email is a postcard to *The Sun* newspaper – reminds governors and trustees alike to be careful and not careless in this domain. Staff in schools are well trained to be careful; missteps still occur.

Boards are well advised to have fact sheets on certain subjects shared amongst board members, for example when external examination and test results are published, or when important decisions have been made public on changes to term times, school hours or admissions arrangements.

Schools and trusts usually refer all enquiries to a common source, but 'fake news' has a habit of turning up and needs prompt countering with the fact sheet. The source of 'know your onions' as a phrase is worth googling, possibly first recorded in 1922 in the US magazine *Harper's Bazaar*.

# ASIDE

## WHAT TO DO?

Staff at some schools within a muti-academy trust have voted to take strike action in response to the trust's leave of absence policy. The policy currently requires staff to take unpaid leave or use their allocated personal leave for medical, dental and other appointments during the school day.

The staff, supported by their unions, argue that they should receive full pay for such absences, citing wellbeing and fairness concerns. The trust leadership maintains that the policy is necessary to manage costs and ensure continuity of education for students.

*The trust board meets to consider its response and next steps. . .*

\*\*\*\*

The long-standing chair of the trust board has dedicated many years of service, providing stability and leadership. However, concerns have been raised by some board members regarding the chair's ability to continue in the role effectively, citing both health and capacity-related issues.

While there is deep respect for the chair's commitment, some governors believe a transition in leadership may be necessary to ensure the board remains effective.

There is hesitation about how to approach the matter without causing distress or disrespect to someone who has given so much to the trust.

*What is the role of the CEO here? Is the board able to discuss this formally at a meeting?. . .*

\*\*\*\*

# LORENZETTI

**Vibrant organisations celebrate strong leadership at all levels.**

*This A–Z is a celebration of good governance. This chapter explores both good and bad governance. The text which follows is explicit that governance and leadership are inextricably interwoven; the narrative is aimed equally at those who govern and those who are governed.*

*The Allegory of Good and Bad Government* is a series of large frescoes painted by Ambrogio Lorenzetti between 1337 and 1339. It is to be viewed in its faded glory in the rooms of Siena's Palazzo Pubblico.

The governing political party of the time commissioned the artist to depict an allegory of 'bad government' featuring the negative dimensions of city life, from assassinations to sacking, violence, poverty and famine. The other allegory depicts the qualities of a 'good government', including visuals such as prosperous cities, cultivated lands, general wellbeing, wealth and joy. An early TV political broadcast if you will.

The painting's overall meaning is abundantly clear: if the city is administered well, the entire population benefits from the administration's successful system of governance.

*Good Government* is represented by a stately figure on a throne; next to whom are the four cardinal virtues: Fortitude, Prudence, Justice and Temperance, joined here by Peace and Magnanimity.

*Bad Government* is represented by a devil-like man, dressed in black and with horns; he is surrounded by allegorical figures representing Cruelty, Discord, War, Fraud, Anger and Tyranny.

You get the picture. Go visit, check opening hours in case under restoration!

## GOOD GOVERNANCE AND LEADERSHIP: SOME ASSERTIONS

**First.** Leadership is a thread that runs through all the other elements in the 'school improvement' process: shared vision, goals and values, sense of school identity, high expectations, efficiency, communications, monitoring, evaluation, professional development, finance.

**Second.** Leadership is exercised at all levels and should never be seen solely or mostly in terms of the head's leadership. These levels include: the board, other members of the senior management team, heads of departments, subject teams, pastoral coordinators, teachers and support colleagues, staff association or union leaders, even the leaders of parent teacher and alumni associations.

**Third.** One level of leadership that is often not considered is that of educational policymakers operating in the bodies or posts at the different levels in which educational policy is made within particular jurisdictions: national or regional education ministers, national education bodies, examining boards, or locally elected committees and their executive arms. The quality of this leadership can have major consequences, both positive and negative, on what happens in schools.

**Fourth.** 'Sustainable leadership' is the golden key. Leadership must not be dependent on one person who may leave, be promoted, die, retire, be sacked or have a breakdown. The key objective must be to ensure that there is such a wide level of commitment to the vision, goals and values of the school – and of experience and expertise in its modes of working – that the institution will carry on regardless, even when the main leader or leaders are changed. This should indeed be part of the definition of a sustainably effective school.

**Fifth.** Leaders must be encouraged to think, and to continue to think, about how they are exercising their leadership roles, to consider the choices that they have in terms of their leadership styles, and to plan to make changes where necessary. We need to be reflective, both as a matter of course in everything we do and in a more planned way in terms of our own self and external evaluation.

**Sixth.** What leaders need above all is to be intelligent. As well as cognitive intelligence, they must also be intelligent in the broader non-cognitive ways. Interpersonal and intrapersonal intelligence, and moral intelligence, are all highly relevant to school leaders.

## BAD GOVERNANCE: SOME ASSERTIONS

**First.** The school improvement process is confused and confusing. There is an absence of high expectations, communication is weak, monitoring and evaluation sporadic, and professional development unfocused.

**Second.** Leadership is over-reliant on too few people and they do not enjoy the confidence of their teams. There can be collusion between executive and senior governors about the realities around them – and, in the case of very poor governance, a refusal to change even when external agencies are urging it.

**Third.** A school or trust, without a clear sense of values and vision, can be swayed by the latest initiative or circular to change its direction, or pander to the loudest voices, or be persuaded to act in ways which are not in the best interests of the local community's children and young people. In extremis, the school can be held to ransom by a tiny minority of powerful, long-standing senior teachers and governors (including Members).

**Fourth.** Leadership that is not shared and nurtured in schools and which can be the victim of single-hero/heroine leaders is destined to falter, sooner or later. Governing boards of course have a fundamental responsibility to ensure that this is not a feature of their schools.

**Fifth.** Schools often change in their intakes of pupils and staff, and in other aspects. Leaders fail to see a school changing around them and fail to adjust. Governors are slow to react, and complacency, then decline, set in. This is an all too familiar cocktail of failing schools.

**Sixth.** Self-awareness and accurate self-assessment; self-management and transparency; social awareness and empathy; relationship management and collaboration – in the dysfunctional school, the absence of these is quickly apparent.

## CODA

Let us be unequivocal here.

When governance goes badly awry, when a group of volunteers cannot see – or choose not to see – a malaise that is affecting students and staff alike, it is time for external agencies to step in. The volunteers need to step down swiftly.

Sadly this can take too long, from a student's standpoint. And when intervention arrives, it can often be spread across local and national newspapers.

It is worth observing that in some of these acute cases it is volunteer board members who 'smell the coffee' quickest and give tirelessly of their time to rescue a context and shape a new future.

Optimistically, more often today than not, through astute review and inspection, leaders and governors are made keenly aware when school improvement needs to accelerate, so that all involved can echo soonest the words of L.P. Hartley: 'The past is a foreign country. They do things differently there.' (Hartley, 1953)

### Advice to chair and principal: seven points to ponder together

1. Do not assume rationality on the part of the people you are dealing with. Remember that we are living post-Freud. Deep emotions can be at work which the people themselves do not begin to understand.

2. Learn to live with the idea that there are multiple perceptions of every situation but do not give up at least on the search for truth. Read almost any great novel. Also, never forget what it is like to feel powerless in the face of authority and be charitable to the perceptions of those who feel themselves to be in this position.

3. Be patient, control your emotions, keep a sense of the unimportance of everything 'in the light of eternity'. Find time for your own interests.

4. Admit mistakes and remember that, in the words of Cardinal de Retz, it is only 'weak people (who) never give way when they ought to' (de Retz, 1717). Be cool, courageous, think quickly and

know when to give way. If deference to those who wish you ill is difficult to stomach, remember the Ethiopian proverb: 'When the great lord passes, the wise peasant bows deeply and silently farts.'

5. Be very explicit about the ethical principles on which you run your schools. Charters and professional codes of conduct that have been developed consultatively, and are constantly referred to and regularly reviewed, can provide communities with the common point of reference that wider contemporary societies often so notably lack.

6. Focus on a limited number of objectives at a time and work hard on them. Remember the Aesop Fable (6th century BC): 'A boy playing in the fields got stung by a nettle. He ran home to his mother, telling her that he had but touched that nasty weed, and it had stung him. "It was just touching it, my boy," said the mother, "that caused it to sting you. The next time you meddle with a nettle, grasp it tightly, and it will do you no hurt."' Do not be half-hearted in tackling difficult issues, says Aesop.

7. Never forget that fate is fickle and the best laid plans may go astray. Fate is unpredictable and the stoic must prepare themselves for it, but also 'it could be much worse'.

---

# ASIDE

## WHAT TO DO?

In a successful trust of primary schools, one of the parent governors wants to help the school by using his contacts in the local business community to review the school's grounds contracts. As a parent governor, he has noticed that the school grounds are not well maintained.

The head of school introduces the governor to the operations manager who explains the tender process in place for large contracts. The governor is unhappy that the school did not meet with the contractor he introduced and complains to the CEO that his views as a governor are not valued.

---

The CEO meets with the governor to clearly explain the role of a local governor and explore how governors can make valuable contributions. The said governor is still not happy and writes a formal complaint to the trust board, and puts the letter on his Facebook page.

*The board meets to discuss. . .*

**\*\*\*\***

The governing body comprises mostly white, middle-aged professionals. There is one governor of colour, a young self-employed single mother. The school staff similarly is mostly white.

As one strategy in a comprehensive approach designed to diversify the staff body, the headteacher is keen to have people of colour on staff recruitment panels. The self-employed governor is keen to sit on a recruitment panel but explains that she will need to be paid for her time.

*What should the governors do?. . .*

**\*\*\*\***

# MINUTES

**'The person who controls the minutes controls the meetings.'**

How would you describe your board and committee meetings?

- The 'Wagner' meeting – of epic length.
- The 'mushroom' meeting – appears suddenly, multiplies rapidly, keeps people in the dark.
- The 'Stonehenge' meeting – it's been a fixture for ages, but nobody knows why.

The old adage runs that a meeting is an event where minutes are taken and hours are wasted. Ask someone who is a regular minute taker and you may or may not hear that refrain. What is true is that the outstanding minute takers I know, literally and metaphorically make an indelible mark – and are major contributors to great governance.

The term 'minute taker' does not do justice to the power and influence they wield; many boards harness the term 'clerk' or 'governance professional'. Whatever nomenclature is used ('clerk' is used in this chapter), 'the person who controls the minutes controls the meetings'. Discuss!

## THE AGENDA AND PAPERS IN GOOD TIME

Once the pattern of meetings and venues is established for the year ahead, the cycle starts. Typically the chair and principal/CEO jointly create the agenda, which is linked to the previous minutes and sets out minor and major items for reporting, recording and discussion. A strong bit of advice is not to overpack the agenda; allow for the tried and tested fact that an item will take longer than you plan time for. The agenda concludes with dates of next meetings, including committee meetings.

A time-honoured habit is to place AOB as a penultimate item. This is a mistake.

Too often someone can raise a matter under this heading, without warning and appropriate background information. What ensues is invariably unsatisfactory, and folk begin to watch the clock nervously. Wise chairs make clear that items on the agenda will always be notified in advance, so that everyone can prepare. Some chairs allow a few minutes at the start of a board meeting, usually as part of welcomes, to give space to anyone who wants to make a personal announcement. We *are* in the people business.

All agendas start with welcomes, recording apologies, reminders about conflicts of interest, approvals of last meeting's minutes, a run through the action tracker – an essential way of following up on previously agreed actions. There are occasional red faces amongst governors when someone has promised to do something and has not had the time. They are forgiven – and will complete for next time.

The clerk will assemble the various papers required for the meeting, compile them into electronic files and dispatch them in good time. What is 'in good time'? Experience suggests a week in advance of a meeting; once agreed, this needs to be kept to. Contemporary best practice is when board members receive the agenda and all papers within one continuous file, with numbered pages, which serves ease of reading and ease of reference at meetings. Voluminous policy files are often sent separately. The clerk checks with all recipients that they have received and can open files.

## HOW DO YOU LIKE YOUR MINUTES?

Well, you play to the strengths of your clerk – and most governing bodies decide what kind of minutes they want to see, kept in similar style through committees and the main board. Do you want a record of what everyone says, the key points made, the action points, a record which captures the flavour of exchanges? My own steer as a chair is 'less is more': please capture the spirit of the meeting; minute the required formalities, the action points, the named individuals who are leading the actions.

Here are three different extracts by way of examples. You may critique each for its strengths and weaknesses. What is important is that, over time, governors agree a format for all minutes that works for them. If there are different minute takers for different meetings, they need to agree a house style. The balance between length and brevity is a fine one.

## Example one

### Safeguarding update

No concerns were raised. The Chair (safeguarding lead) and Director of Education continue to meet half termly to address any issues and to ensure that safeguarding remains effective throughout the organisation.

All were reminded to complete annual safeguarding refresher training.

### Policy Review: Trustees' Expenses Policy and Safeguarding Policy

The Board reviewed and approved the Trustees' Expense Policy.

It was agreed that the expenses procedure is robust and aligns with the Charity Commission's guidance.

The Board reviewed and approved the Child Protection and Safeguarding Policy. It was noted that it aligns with statutory updates.

### Remuneration Committee new Terms of Reference

The Board considered and approved the revised Terms of Reference and noted it would be renamed the People and Remuneration Committee.

### Risk Register

The Board noted the Risk Register and was satisfied that the organisation has appropriate systems and controls in place.

- The issue regarding science laboratories redevelopment could not happen under the new procedures in place.
- It was agreed that reputational risk is embedded in the other risks, alongside the extra risk about alignment with stakeholders.

- The Finance and Audit Committee will address the risk of cyber attack. JD offered to join the discussion.
- Cyber-security training was recommended to the Education Committee.

• • • •

## Example two

**Year 11 data:** continued prediction of 45-50% 4+ Eng/maths, with a strong focus on 18 students who are critical to achieving the combined.

**Safeguarding:** external review on 18th March discussed – members asked about follow up on DSL supervision and an SCR query – both resolved promptly. Board pleased to read summary of changed culture in school.

**Coaching programme:** excellent progress, really having an impact on a number of staff who are enjoying the process of improving their teaching. A number of colleagues have asked if they can contribute to the programme. Wider impact on whole-school culture: corridors, dining room, etc. Tighter discipline has led to small rise in exclusions.

**Site management:** gradual improvements; from Easter, 3 staff on site should make a significant difference.

**Staffing from Easter:** new SENCO, music, maths, Director of Sports. First time in five years a term will start with school fully staffed.

**Transition plan:** September 2024, Year 7 numbers stand at 128 allocated, against backcloth of falling pupil numbers in town.

**Attendance for students and staff:** data sheets discussed. 'No stone unturned'. Year 7 is 2% below county average. Board still concerned about Year 11 attendance in particular.

• • • •

## Example three

### Update on actions:

TS – We have been discussing this. We wanted to ask the Committee if quantifying reviews as a metric is helpful or not. We could report back in terms of metric as to how much has been completed.

DE – Outcomes is what we are looking for as well as processes being done. How would you know that schools are safe?

JI – Agree but imagine this would be difficult to do.

HR – Ultimately, we need to stay focused on outcomes.

CT – We need to know that students are safe in school and involve wider agencies that are crucial in the wider safeguarding in student's lives.

LJ – We could compare how many MARFs (Multi-Agency Referral Forms) there are compared to last year. Why is there a drop? Has there been a change in culture? We could look a bit deeper at this. It is not a measurement as such but gives us a way to be preventative.

LJ – Using data a bit more creatively – not only what it tells us but what it does not tell us.

JI – Comparative trends – a second stage analysis of what the numbers are telling us.

DE – There are still some variables that could be tracked – bullying for example. We need to carry on thinking about what data we collect.

CT – We will keep this as an action and keep working on it.

## THE FOLLOW-UP

When you ask a group of senior students what makes for a great teacher, they invariably comment on the teacher who marks their work promptly and returns it to them with next steps clearly delineated. Talk to chairs and headteachers and they say the same about minutes: promptly drafted, checked and circulated so everyone knows what follow-up is expected, by whom and by when.

In addition to the clerk's prompt follow-up, many headteachers and CEOs will send out a short email to colleagues, summing up the key points of a meeting. This quality of timely communication builds trust. Here is an extract from a trust chair to all headteachers:

- We were generously hosted by Kavita in a school with an outstanding cultural mix and harmony, so impressive.
- We welcomed new members Narayan and Lisa to the board.
- We agreed we shall conduct a board self-review; clerk will send further details.
- We signed off, subject to a few final numbers and typos, the outstanding Annual Report. Please share it locally.

## THE CLERK'S VOICE

Conversations with practising clerks on how they see their role are worth having – the chair might do this informally or more formally on an annual basis, whatever both parties feel most comfortable with.

To answer the exam question at the start of this chapter: most clerks would attest that they do not control the meeting but that they need to step in if the meeting starts to stray. Confidence for the clerk to say something there and then if they feel it is necessary is essential, as often after the meeting has closed it is too late. The clerk's good rapport with the board underpins everything.

Furthermore, clerks affirm that they need to keep on top of legislation and policy so that the board is confident that the information they receive from them is correct. They usually agree that clerking is not difficult if you know your stuff but that it always surprises them how reticent people are if they are asked to 'take notes' at a meeting.

To close a chapter which celebrates the work of many, many thousands of clerks to governing bodies across the country, in the words of one outstanding practitioner: 'When I was studying for my certificate in academy governance, my tutor told us – you need to be serious but that does not have to mean solemn. This relieved me as I do have difficulty remaining solemn!'

# ASIDE

## WHAT TO DO?

Following a review of the cost of the school uniform, most governors are keen to significantly review the school's uniform requirements, replacing blazers, shirts and ties with polo shirts and sweatshirts. This would make the uniform significantly cheaper.

A vocal minority of governors take to social media to protest this change.

The headteacher and senior leaders are also very much against this suggestion, saying that it would have a detrimental impact on the school's image and the behaviour of the students.

*The governors have a special meeting...*

\*\*\*\*

The school is under new leadership. The headteacher has commissioned a robust school review using an external review partner. The review has highlighted that the school is significantly underperforming and robust action is needed. This was feedback that the headteacher had anticipated.

The headteacher makes the decision to share this with the chair of governors as a key player in the school. The chair reacts emotionally, asking for a meeting between the headteacher, deputies, chair and vice-chair of governors. During the meeting the chair and vice-chair are both emotional and confrontational. The two deputies are very upset following the meeting.

*Who does what, by way of next steps?...*

\*\*\*\*

# NOLAN

### Seven elegant principles of public life worth observing at every turn.

Most of the change we think we see in life
Is due to truths being in and out of favor.
As I sit here, and often times, I wish
I could be monarch of a desert land
I could devote and dedicate forever
To the truths we keep coming back and back to.

*The Black Cottage* by Robert Frost

When good governance permeates the everyday workings of an organisation, it is seen as a river running deeply through all that is happening 'front of house' and 'behind the scenes'. A school, college or trust may happily never experience a blip with its governance, but when there are significant concerns, it is more than likely that one of the principles below has been compromised.

The seven principles of public life were first set out by Lord Nolan in 1995 (Committee on Standards in Public Life, 1995) and are included in the Ministerial Code. They have roundly stood the test of time. They provide an invaluable touchstone in the good conduct of those who govern and those who are governed in a wide range of private, public and third sector contexts.

The principles are worth a board revisiting for a few moments' reflection, and pause, on an annual basis.

Contestably, they are a recipe for a good life well lived; and which of us can say with candour that we are unfailingly perfect with regard to these principles? To err is to be human. Or, in the infamous words of fourth century philosopher Saint Augustine: 'Lord, make me pure but not yet'.

Let us take each in turn, acknowledging degrees of overlap.

**1. Selflessness**: *Holders of public office should act solely in terms of the public interest.*

Sitting, standing and walking alongside many hundreds of governors, my experience is that they join a board in a resolute spirit of selflessness. What actually motivates one person may be different from another, but what unites is that governors wish to serve the public interest. In a given local community, they put themselves forward in the belief that others will trust them to think and act wisely in the best interests of the school. Extrinsic and intrinsic motivation are to be weighed here.

**2. Integrity:** *Holders of public office must avoid placing themselves under any obligation to people or organisations that might try inappropriately to influence them in their work. They should not act or take decisions in order to gain financial or other material benefits themselves, their family, or their friends. They must declare and resolve any interests and relationships.*

There are three thoughtfully worded aspects at play here, and 'integrity' can readily be viewed all too subjectively. First, governors are there to listen to various viewpoints as part of their insight/oversight role. It is their independence that is valued and not to be compromised by being 'obliged' to a particular person, pressure group or, indeed, business interest.

Second, the avoidance of 'material benefits' is fundamental. Sadly when this aspect fails (sometimes linked to family and friends) adverse publicity and broken trust are quick to follow. Transparency is the watchword; *how* things are perceived needs to be carefully thought through.

Third, wise decision making is rapidly compromised when personal interests and relationships get in the way; all governors need to be vigilant here.

**3. Objectivity:** *Holders of public office must act and take decisions impartially, fairly and on merit, using the best evidence and without discrimination or bias.*

Experience across most governing and trustee boards would indicate that colleagues do act with due impartiality, considering issues carefully and fairly, and weighing thoughtfully the merits of the information presented. One person's hunch can be another person's prejudice; one person's objectivity can be another's subjectivity – that's to be human in our everyday dealings. Yet widespread evidence indicates that there is a consistent effort by governors to act without discrimination or bias.

**4. Accountability:** *Holders of public office are accountable to the public for their decisions and actions and must submit themselves to the scrutiny necessary to ensure this.*

Strong individual and collective accountability permeate effective boards. Balancing the budget, dealing fairly with employees, safeguarding the best interests of children and young people – these three aspects in any context are probably where most governors feel high visibility in being held to account for their actions.

Confident boards welcome audits and external reviews which scrutinise their ways of working and decisions.

**5. Openness:** *Holders of public office should act and take decisions in an open and transparent manner. Information should not be withheld from the public unless there are clear and lawful reasons for so doing.*

In popular media parlance, the question to politicians when something goes awry is: 'who knew what when?' Hindsight is always a glorious thing. Competent governance seeks to be as transparent as it can reasonably be, mindful that confidentiality has an important part to play when staff and students are involved.

In extremis, court cases often focus on information being withheld or disclosed at the wrong time by the wrong people. Chairs and executive leaders working thoughtfully in tandem can reduce, though never eliminate, the likelihood of error. Legal advice needs sometimes to be sought – arguably an increasing feature of contemporary society.

**6. Honesty**: *Holders of public office should be truthful.*

Whilst high profile cases of dishonesty pepper the educational press at intervals, it is overwhelmingly the case that those who put themselves forward to be trustees and governors embody an honest and truthful approach to their volunteer work. Indeed, how could it be otherwise when at the heart of schools are values around probity and decency, which staff and pupils live out every day?

What is at work here is a high level of mutual accountability.

**7. Leadership:** *Holders of public office should exhibit these principles in their own behaviour. They should actively promote and robustly support the principles and be willing to challenge poor behaviour wherever it occurs.*

Our seventh principle is intended to echo back through the preceding six. In the same way that all teachers are leaders when it comes to modelling behaviours and values to those they teach, all governors and trustees are role models in their communities. When any sign of 'poor behaviour' surfaces, peer governors are in my experience very quick to exert proper influence to identify such occurrences. And this often takes personal bravery, not to be underestimated.

The chair's role is critical here, primus inter pares, often working skilfully through chairs of committees and with the senior executive. There will always be 'outliers'. *How* these people and incidents are managed is often a true test of fine governance.

*****

The Nolan principles are an attractive articulation of what civic society expects of its public servants, paid or volunteers. Great organisations thrive on promoting and embedding the seven principles, their people intuitively practising honesty, openness and objectivity.

Of course it's a rare institution that does not experience a breakdown in trust or is questioned about its accountability systems at some point. Good governance acts swiftly on these occasions, holds its hands up, reviews keenly 'lessons learned' – and moves forwards, confident in its actions and next steps.

# ASIDE

## WHAT TO DO?

Due to a fall in school funding, a significant restructure is needed across the school. This includes a recommendation to remove a key post of specialist music in the primary school. An alternative option to provide high quality music provision through the local music services is part of the restructure presentation.

During the initial governing body meeting to look at the restructure, there are many differing views around the music provision in the school. Music has always had a high profile within the school and the local community.

A group of parents are informed by the parent governor that music is likely to be cut from the curriculum. They write to the chair of governors, and send a copy to the local newspaper.

*Governors meet to discuss a way forward...*

****

At the end of her first year as a new member of the governing body, a parent governor voices her concerns, in a full meeting, about the chair of governors. She says that he does not provide sufficient challenge to the school's leadership team and does not take into account the views of all governors.

*How should the chair of governors respond?...*

AND

One of the members of the people committee has significant HR experience in his own role. He has, however, missed two consecutive meetings without sending his apologies and has not responded to an email and a phone call from the Governance Professional.

*What steps should the committee now take?...*

****

# OPTIMISM

**Optimism radiates from confident school leaders and board chairs.**

## A    EIGHT MAXIMS FOR SCHOOL LEADERS

### 1. Leave them with a smile on their face

Leading schools requires taking important decisions at regular intervals. Getting the right tone with colleagues matters, especially when leaders have to convey difficult messages. There is a real knack to 'telling it like it is' and still leaving the member of staff in good spirits. Accomplished heads manage to get this right most of the time, and learn quickly when they make a mistake. 'It's not what I'm saying that matters. It's what you are hearing'.

### 2. Less is more

In the face of daunting bureaucracy, wise heads know how to cut to the chase. Emails, reports, letters of complaint, advisory notes, safeguarding updates, financial spreadsheets – the sheer volume of material can threaten to swamp. A hallmark of thoughtful leadership is the ability to sift at pace, with an eye for the important detail. Crafting one side of A4, with the right words in the right order, is practical and accessible for any audience, whether governor, inspector or parent.

### 3. It's not what's in the diary that kills you, it's what is not in the diary

Headteachers' diaries can be proverbial bombsites. Everyone wants to see the head, right now. If you are not very careful, the urgent consumes the important. But with a full list of scheduled diary commitments, along comes something really urgent. The best heads have developed creative solutions to potential diary crashes, usually involving a skilled secretary, willing deputies and the occasional 'white lies'. Time juggling is part of the job: live to fight another day.

### 4. Leaders enable…managers control

It is a natural inclination early in a manager's career to want to control. You've been promoted so show what you can do. Observing skilled middle managers is to see them starting 'tight' then being willing to 'loosen'. And it's certainly what great heads do: appoint the right people in the right places and let them flourish in a climate of measured risk. The average manager seeks to control colleagues, while the confident leader is quite content for others to shine and to take the plaudits.

### 5. Easier to beg forgiveness than seek permission

Not every leader subscribes to this principle of management. But show me a great school leader who regularly seeks permission rather than following deep professional instincts, and I'll show you a school that risks faltering. Students get one chance, so no head compromises that basic tenet. But principled and values-led decision making, inclusive of staff and students, creates vibrant teaching and learning communities. A leader does not want people looking over their shoulders all the time. Instead of seeking permission, they occasionally have to say sorry.

### 6. A quick 'no' or a slow 'yes'

The old headteacher adage of 'never say yes in a corridor' rings true for many school leaders. Staff often want instant decisions from headteachers – and there's a place for those, for example in certain health and safety contexts. But wisdom suggests that a little time pondering with colleagues will lead to a better course of actions. Judicious timing in headship is crucial, so better a quick 'no' and slow 'yes'. The alternative can be 'command and reverse', which is a recipe for confusion.

### 7. An email is a postcard to *The Sun*

In politics, so in headship, timing and communication are everything. Contemporary headship is played out against a backcloth of 24-hour media, X and Instagram. Pupils and parents can turn a petty drama into a crisis at the flick of a thumb. Heads today spend a disproportionate amount of time picking up the pieces of poorly worded emails. Good schools and wise leaders have established clear protocols for all staff when responding to social media. Caveat emptor has become sender beware.

### 8. Graveyards are full of indispensable people

Spending time alongside heads in schools, helping them see afresh their daily routines, is endlessly fascinating. The best amongst them stay resolutely focused on the students they serve. Equally, they are highly skilled in identifying the next generation of leaders. Succession planning informs heads' everyday working, nudging potential future leaders to follow their instincts, to believe in their potential, to carve out ways of doing which challenge prevailing orthodoxies. Today's agile school leader remembers Prime Minister David Cameron's parting parliamentary words: 'I was the future once'.

## B    EIGHT MAXIMS FOR CHAIRS OF BOARDS

### 1. Watch the clock

If you do nothing else as a chair of meetings, start and finish on time. It's surprising how many meetings contrive to have a slow start – and then drag on way beyond the planned finishing time so that headteachers think their lives are slipping away as evening darkness arrives. Some chairs opt for timed business which is tricky if certain items end up requiring more time for debate. Better to be flexible in the moment but resolute about making up time and sometimes postponing an item for another day. And do not let the executive talk too much!

### 2. Speak clearly, listen keenly, smile often

Your fellow governors want you to lead at the top of the meeting, making them feel valued and welcome. They want to know what you think, but do not speak first on every item. They want to know that you are listening keenly to all views – before summarising and moving to a decision. If you are a better talker than a listener, plan with a colleague governor to restrain you through eye contact. If you are a better listener than a talker, do not leave your colleagues guessing. The timely smile is worth a hundred words. The judicious use of wit and humour is always welcome.

### 3. Plan B can be better than Plan A

You and the executive may have set out to present Plan A convincingly, and you may be absolutely on the right track. Do not hold back in orchestrating compelling arguments in favour of a planned course of action. Rehearse and revisit and review. Yet, always have a smidgen of doubt. Be prepared for fellow governors to see an alternative fork in the road. Listen to their arguments, consider their interpretations of facts and figures. Plan B may well emerge as a better route. That's not defeat – that's a triumph of listening, transparency and effective governance.

### 4. Let someone else have the last word

Chairs begin and end discussions on items at a meeting. That's what others expect – and is usually effective practice. Occasionally it is worth breaking that mould. Feelings may have been running high during the discussion of a sensitive item. There may have been agreeable disagreements. As chair, you do not have to have the final word, offering the mot juste. It might just be adroit to pass that torch to someone else on the board, if you are confident they will choose their words carefully, and smile not scowl when doing so. The clerk can give a helpful unopinionated summary.

### 5. Unite all differences intact

It may be why you were elected or nominated as chair – your ability to bring people together. Nudging folk towards a consensus they did not think was possible, uniting all differences intact – that can be a challenge, but an outcome worth pushing for. You may not get thanked immediately – but in the fullness of time, the chair's wisdom will be appreciated. And here's a question: should you ever move to a vote if you really do not need to? Arguably, votes divide. Folk leave a room feeling they have been defeated – not what you want with a group of volunteers. Affirm rather than vote.

### 6. Wear your knowledge lightly

The chair may well be the most knowledgeable governor in the room, perhaps through years of service, perhaps through working closely with the executive prior to the meeting, perhaps through personal and professional experience. By comparison, other members of the board may still be learning their way into the organisation or indeed into being a governor or trustee. Climb inside their shoes, see the meeting from their viewpoint. Use your in-depth knowledge yet wear it lightly – and be happy to be corrected when you make a mistake.

## 7. If you stand still long enough you become a radical

Over time, trends and fashions and opinions change. The zeitgeist five years ago may not be the same as today. You may have become chair when certain educational orthodoxies prevailed, but those orthodoxies are now different. Ask yourself where you stand – socially, politically, educationally – in relation to current thinking. Have you stood still? Have you shifted? Wise chairs know themselves well. They remember that if they stand still long enough they become radicals – at least, as perceived by others...

## 8. Blink! Life goes faster than you think

How long have you served on the board, and how long as chair? When is your sell-by date do you think? Will someone nudge you? Research into effective chairs and their lengths of service is predictably inconclusive: three years may suit some boards in certain modes, ten years may suit others. Skilled chairs will take counsel from trusted board members and executive leaders about when is the best moment to pass on the board leadership baton. Plan your exit strategy for the right moment for the organisation; think about likely successors and offer your opinion. Leave with no backward glance.

# ASIDE

## WHAT TO DO?

The governor with responsibility for governor development/training outlined a plan for all governors 12 months ago. Since this meeting, however, she has not shared any further training plans and one governor has already resigned quoting a lack of support.

*Who should do what now?. . .*

**∗∗∗∗**

The headteacher has brought an updated policy on the use of mobile phones to governors. This gains broad support from the governing body.

However, a parent governor is adamant that the policy should be changed and says that it is her role to act as a representative of the parental body. To this end, she presents governors with a petition with signatures from over 100 parents to support her case.

*How should the governing body respond?. . .*

**∗∗∗∗**

# PEOPLE

**Capable trustees never lose sight of the fact that they are in the people business.**

One of the memorable quotes attributed to Howard Schultz, founder and CEO of Starbucks runs: 'We are not in the coffee business serving people, but in the people business serving coffee' (Shultz, 1999).

There can be few 'businesses' in existence that are not fundamentally 'people businesses'. Thus, trustees and governors are usually pretty experienced in dealing with people from their own professional and, of course, personal lives. Indeed, it is that very range of experiences which make them effective governors, able to enrich debate with their reflections from other settings and workplaces.

What often attracts volunteers to work in schools and colleges in particular is that they enjoy being in the company of children and young people, glimpsing the attitudes and sensibilities of the young generation. Governors sometimes quip that the problems are never with the pupils, just the staff. All things are relative.

Proverbs 29 in the King James Bible affirms that 'where there is no vision, the people perish'. One key aspect of governance is helping shape, promote and sustain the vision of an organisation which brings together young people, staff, colleagues around the school/trust and those who govern.

## CHILDREN AND YOUNG PEOPLE

Governors are more than likely to live in the community serving the school, so they see first-hand, up-close and every day the children and young people, going to and from school, getting on and off public transport, popping into the local shops. Impressions are formed, usually positive and occasionally negative. Governors rightly bring those observations and impressions to meetings and to discussions – in the best traditions of local voices, they *are* the community eyes and ears.

Commonly, governors will comment on what they see as the successes of young people, as presented in headteachers' reports and newsletters – and what they might be hearing from their own children and children's friends. Items in meetings that ask governors to reflect on student's triumphs are invariably popular items and enable all governors to feel optimistic about everyday life in the school. These are the easy, comfortable and pleasurable aspects of being a governor – and should never be taken for granted. Excellence is rooted in what we repeatedly do.

From time to time, headteachers will ask governors to consider instances of 'students behaving badly', some serious, some less so. Governors who are parents are especially careful not to be judging others, but may well be drawn into wider discussions about actions to be taken by the leaders. That goes with the responsibilities of the role and can demand much of a volunteer in terms of respect for confidentiality. On occasion, governors have to recuse themselves though potential conflict of interest.

School leaders are usually expert at guiding governors through protocols related to disciplinary matters. Governors are rightly advised to read carefully documentation that is given to them, hopefully *key* documentation rather than an overload of unnecessary paperwork.

There is no doubt that governors and trustees take great pleasure in hearing about, discussing and subsequently celebrating children and young people's achievements: in classrooms, on sports fields, in competitions and especially in contexts that take them out into the community. Equally, they recognise that there are occasions when, by the very nature of dealing with young people, harder conversations need to be entered into. School leaders invariably value the advice of trusted governors.

# STAFF

One key to successful schools is the extent to which teaching and support staff see governors as a positive force for good in the way they govern and promote what pupils and staff are engaged in every day. What is shared is a healthy mutual respect and a clarity of understanding about where matters are operational and where they have governance implications. Wise headteachers, trust leaders and chairs of boards model the terms of engagement.

Some staff are of course elected as governors on school boards and have a particular role to play, bringing the staff voice to the table. Used well, the staff voice is vital to the smooth running of the school; misused, it can be harmful and sometime require a chair of governors and headteacher to counsel accordingly.

In many contexts, governors will offer their services to be alongside staff, in classrooms, on playing fields and joining school visits. Their volunteer time and expertise are highly valued. It is also an opportunity for them to talk to staff about conditions of service and other employee matters, which in turn inform governors' decision making over budgets and current and future staffing needs.

It is the to-fro positive interaction between staff and governors over time which can serve a school community so well. There are invariably times when difficulties arise. And when matters go wrong, it can be disproportionately disruptive to good relations and relationships.

Yet if trust is an integral feature, then staff will respect sometimes problematic staffing matters which governors have to address. Appropriate transparency, honesty and respect for confidentiality are sometimes uneasy companions. Handled well by leaders, staff and governors can manage their way through challenging situations and come out the other side, with enhanced respect for each other's respective roles and responsibilities.

## THE TEAM AROUND THE SCHOOL

Whether with a maintained school or in the context of a multi-academy trust, governors engage with a range of colleagues beyond the school.

This will include education advisers, estate managers, HR staff, IT support and much besides.

Forging positive relationships with 'the team around the school' is vital to deliver effective governance: you never know when each may need to call upon the other, often working alongside one another in committees or in full board meetings.

Individual governors may be tasked with working closely with members of the wider team, so these relationships are important.

When additional classrooms projects, a new IT system or a refurbishing of a kitchen and canteen are the focus, it may well be the case that governors' own professional expertise is brought into play. Good boards these days are ever mindful of conflicts of interest; equally they are savvy enough to play to governors' passions, strengths and interests in the best service of value for money and delivering enhanced educational provision.

## FELLOW BOARD MEMBERS

In smaller communities it may be the case that governors know each other well and see one another often in that community. For other governors and trustees, they may only meet through (virtual) committees and at board meetings. Either way, relationships build and friendships are formed, united by the common purpose of good governance.

Away-days, socials and pre-meeting refreshments are often features of developing a board's climate and ways of being and working together – and these are not to be under-valued. Governors understanding one another as people and what makes them tick is a vital ingredient – and certainly makes a difference when thorny issues arise in the formality of the meetings. Deepening mutual respect makes for better decision making – and usually a calmer time for the chair and the executive leader.

****

It is instructive to observe the development of a board over time, how its members affirm, debate, interpret, disagree; and how they welcome new members to their gatherings and assist in their settling in. Chairs of governors – with the executive – set the tone and the scene; true fellowship unfolds.

To be part of a governing board which exudes rightful confidence in itself, in fellow governors, in the chair and the executive is to be part of something special as a volunteer. Complacency settling in would be almost unthinkable. Invariably, that degree of mutual respect and trust is a guarantee of very good governance – the school, the college, the trust is then the rich beneficiary.

---

# ASIDE

## WHAT TO DO?

The lead governor for SEND has a child with special educational needs and has arranged several meetings with the special educational needs coordinator (SENCO).

The latter has complained to the headteacher, saying that the parent has misused her position as governor in an attempt to influence the level of support her child receives.

The headteacher has raised this with the chair of governors.

*How should the chair respond?...*

****

One of the governors is very well connected in the local community, which brings many benefits to the school, including free access to facilities at the local cricket club.

However, your attention has recently been drawn to a number of widely seen social media posts, including one from a cricket club social, in which she is visibly very drunk.

*What should the chair of governors do?...*

****

---

# QUESTIONS

**Asking great questions – and listening keenly to the answers – are hallmarks of successful governing boards.**

Answers tend to have a pretty short shelf life. Answers are relevant to particular problems at particular moments. You can agree or disagree with them.

In contrast, a good question can last forever.

Dip into a handbook for small business owners (and many governors are) and the following seven questions are key starting points:

1. What problem does your business solve?
2. How does your business generate net income?
3. Which parts of your business are not profitable?
4. Is your cash flow positive each month?
5. What is your pricing strategy and why?
6. How effectively do employees generate revenue?
7. What is your customer retention rate?

Dip into a comparable handbook for trustees of a charity (and governors are often involved in other charities) and these questions come top:

1. What effect is the current economic climate having on our charity and its activities?
2. What effect is the economic climate having on our donors?
3. Are we financially strong enough to sustain our development plans?

4. Have we reviewed our contractual commitments, office leases, rental agreements?

5. How can we make best use of permanent endowment investments we hold?

6. Have we considered collaborating with other charities?

Governors from different walks of life bring their own questions to a school or trust. Some of the questions above are worth adapting to the educational workplace. Executive leaders benefit from being asked to 'climb inside another's shoes', to listen to views which come from a contrasting professional mindset and skillset.

## QUESTIONS TO SELF

As a governor you are no doubt regularly asking yourself whether you think you are adding value when you turn up at meetings. We all do that as part of our volunteering spirit. It's always worth reflecting on the positives before you let doubt creep in. If you are regularly contributing to committees and to board discussions then the executive and the chair will surely have acknowledged those contributions.

It is also worth thinking back to when you first joined the board and reflect how much has been achieved over that period: whether it has been delivering new classrooms, expanding admissions, the introduction of an exciting curriculum programme, or sustaining high quality education for all and thus achieving a very healthy inspection/review outcome.

The self-review example on page 193 is worth a look. Does your governing body conduct such an audit of its members on an annual or biannual basis?

## QUESTIONS IN MEETINGS

Accomplished teachers affirm that high quality questioning in classrooms lies at the heart of their trade. It is not only what you ask but *how* you ask students, how you build a series of questions to help them understand new knowledge and skills. We remember what we have to think deeply about – and we cannot write what we cannot say.

In early years, skilled teachers are asking why is the water flowing quickly, why do these words rhyme, why do these numbers go in a sequence? As children move up through primary school, the teacher starts to work at a different level of sophistication: why do we use this mathematical formula here, why did peoples emigrate, why do we apply this fair test? And moving to older students, the questions become more demanding, with less obvious right and wrong answers: why (do we think) did this war leader act as he did, why did this character murder his wife, why did this painter use this technique, why not combine these two chemicals?

(Blatchford, 2023)

Limits of time caused by over-busy agendas sometime inhibit productive discussions, the chair always has an eye on the clock. If there is a serious topic requiring interrogation and it is important that all voices are heard, then thinking and speaking space must be created. This then allows for thoughtful questions, answers and reflections around the Harkness oval table.

Asking what may appear tough and searching questions – with a twinkle in the eye and not a frown on the face – is what good governance demands, at least some of the time. The chair is there to moderate, summarise and move the debate on to a fruitful conclusion.

Where a supportive climate of mutual trust and adherence to the Nolan principles of public life (see pages 88–90) are in evidence across a board, those demanding questions enrich decision making.

It was Mark Twain who wrote: 'To a man who only has a hammer, everything he encounters begins to look like a nail.' To those of us steeped in education ways of doing, in lifelong professional jargon, in the commerce of corridors and classrooms – it can be difficult to see our own world a little differently. This is where the dumb question matters, and can lead to a collective rethink of established orthodoxies:

- Why do we have a one-week half-term?
- Do teachers need to be in school when they are not teaching?

- Why do we employ cover teachers in classrooms when we have excellent private study areas?
- Why does the building close through the summer holidays?

During my years as a headteacher I served on a brand-new prison's board of visitors for a period. The governor would frequently ask me to pose what he called was 'the question I am blind to'. In another context, while serving on the board of a major theatre company, the distinguished and energetic chair used to encourage members to ask 'the questions you think your children would ask'.

It is the governor/trustee who is less steeped in education-speak who can ask the dumb question nicely. It proves not so dumb after all. It is the reason why governing boards at their best benefit from a wide range of perspectives and life experiences. In turn, the executive comes to value that sharp questioning even if it might make them squirm intellectually, just for a moment. (See also **Boards**, page 9)

## LISTENING AND ACHIEVING CONSENSUS

Aphorisms on listening – there are plenty out there. The question is: do those who talk too much read, hear and learn from them?

'Listen to what others have to say. When you speak, you're only repeating things you already know. When you listen, you learn.'

'Being president is like running a cemetery: you've got a lot of people under you and nobody is listening.'

'The opposite of talking isn't listening. The opposite of talking is waiting.'

'Every good conversation you've ever had where you come away feeling lifted, almost certainly the other person was listening carefully.'

Governors will know from their own families and workplaces that there are people who talk a lot and do not really listen; there are those who are good listeners and are shy to offer an opinion; and there are those who are both good listeners and thoughtful talkers. That's life.

Whichever kind of talker and listener we might be, we try to be more balanced, certainly as we get older. This matters in family, social and work groups – and it certainly matters in the context of good governance.

The chair can only do so much, working with the raw material they have! Achieving consensus *is* important, and that relies on all of us learning to give a little, to listen keenly, to appreciate and value different perspectives. If the meeting requires extra time to reach that point of consensus, the wise chair will come to that conclusion and act accordingly. Holding an additional one-topic, one-hour meeting has its place in confident governance.

# ASIDE
## WHAT TO DO?

The school has been through some difficult times recently but is now improving rapidly. Data demonstrates clearly that standards of behaviour and quality of education are both substantially better than they were a year ago.

Three governors have children in the school, and those governors are all sceptical about the data. In meetings, they openly question the validity of the data because they say the anecdotal evidence from their children does not support the narrative of improvement.

The chair and headteacher decide to make this a substantive item at an upcoming meeting of the board.

*What follows?...*

****

The principal spends a long time preparing for governors' meetings, producing a very substantial report which is sent out at least a week in advance. At the meetings, it is clear from the questions governors ask that they have not read the report.

The chair routinely asks the principal to 'elaborate' on sections of the report that governors are interested in, which in reality means reading and explaining that section to the meeting. Subsequent discussions are chaired badly, with repetitive points being given space and obvious chances to summarise and move forward being missed. Consequently, meetings can last for well over three hours.

The principal shares her frustrations with the chair and they agree to have a main item on the subject of reports and governors' reading of them.

*What issues emerge at the meeting?. . .*

****

# RISKS

## An acute eye on balancing risks is ever on the governance agenda.

'Risk' is an intriguing word in the English language. It is a fact that when we are successful in something everyone is happy to congratulate us. On the other hand, failure can attract pretty sharp looks and comments. Writer G.K. Chesterton contrarily observed: 'If a thing is worth doing, it is worth doing badly.' (Chesterton, 1910) But that is not how the world normally sees things.

Interviews with successful performers and business folk are peppered with quotable lines on the subject of risk – and different cultures in different eras see the concept of risk differently.

Great deeds are usually wrought at great risks.

Herodotus

Prophesy is a good line of business, but it is full of risks.

Mark Twain

As a goalkeeper, you have to take risks even though at times you make mistakes.

Victor Valdes

Everybody fails, it's no big deal. It's what being human is. Don't let that stop you from taking risks.

Katty Kay

One hour of life, crowded to the full with glorious action, and filled with noble risks, is worth whole years of those mean observances of paltry decorum.

Walter Scott

We live in a risk-averse age, society awash with regulations and 'do-nots'. Even measured risk-taking is frowned upon and the CYA ('cover-your-ass') mentality is everywhere, whether in the public, private or not-for-profit sectors. The ambulance-chasing lawyers; the advertisements that encourage dispute first, reconciliation second; the often laughable claims for trivial damages to property – this is the zeitgeist.

In the education sphere come the parents who complain to Ofsted and threaten headteachers with lawyers for the most petty of incidents; employees who search for spurious reasons to claim financial compensation for minor matters which in a previous era would have been seen for what they are – minor matters. This is not to deny a proper right of reply; it is to question whether society has the balance right in so many walks of life.

Schools anywhere in the world, in essence, comprise a building and the people within it. Schools are as simple and as complex as that, whether you are looking at a primary school in Cornwall, an all-through campus in Manchester or one of the fascinating boat schools in Vietnam (you can read about the latter in this article on the *Vietnam+* website: https://en.vietnamplus.vn/first-floating-school-in-vietnam-put-into-operation-post59425.vnp).

How a school is funded, how internal organisation works, how it is staffed, what is taught and who attends – these aspects follow. Thus it is that governance is principally concerned with three major areas of risk, the triumvirate of: people, buildings, finance. Take a look at any board's colour-coded risk register, with its risks and mitigations carefully set out, and these are the headline items.

# A    PEOPLE

In the way that a nation's leaders say that their first duty is the safety of their people, wise governance places the health, safety and wellbeing of its people top of the risk register.

In today's world it is very rare for a school not to be absolutely 'on it' with regard to keeping children safe. I taught in Pimlico School, London in the 1970s and once discovered a photographer who had wandered on to the premises to take pictures of our wonderful murals painted by students – those were more innocent days.

Arrive at any school campus and you are struck – and sometimes stuck – by security at gates.

Once through those and reception awaits. Having pressed the buzzer you are in and appropriate checks and coloured lanyards ensue – the colour of the lanyard dictates whether you can be accompanied or unaccompanied. You are asked to read the safeguarding leaflet, fire evacuation and lockdown procedures. There are photos and names of who students, staff and visitors should report to if they have safeguarding concerns. A nominated safeguarding governor keeps a special eye on this domain.

Around any school one is usually, not always, struck by the site team's attention to detail over clean environments – and in my lifetime in schools I have never seen or heard of a case of food poisoning coming out of a kitchen. School canteens are quite the safest places to eat in the kingdom. Striking too in schools is the keen awareness children and young people have of the importance of clean classrooms and corridors, though fine intentions are not always met in actions; many toilets in secondary schools remain challenging in this regard.

As a governor walking the school, this is what one sees – and it is good to feed back this generally positive picture to leaders; it certainly helps board members feel confident when reviewing risk registers.

Staff's conditions of service in relation to their workplace are equally important for governors to examine. Most staffrooms today are fit for purpose and some make a point of being quite special in their design and comfort. Leaders look carefully at light, airy and temperature-controlled classrooms for teachers to teach in and students to study well in.

Not to be overlooked are the office spaces provided for the many support staff who make a significant contribution to any contemporary school. Their health, safety and wellbeing matter the same as that of the students and the teachers.

First and last on the people risk register: recruitment and retention. While children are generally a captive audience, securing high quality teachers to put in front of them is not a given. Often top of a school's or trust's risk register is loss of very good staff at every level and what mitigation the board is implementing. There can be few board meetings that take place without leaders talking about capacity issues. Board members often observe: 'you should see just what challenges we are facing in our own workplace'.

# B    ESTATE

For a governing body this applies to one set of buildings on a campus. For trustees this may involve a focus on 20 different sites.

Leaking flat roofs, broken windows, rotting windowsills, fractured gutters, a Forth Bridge redecoration schedule, potholes in the drives, subsidence on the playing fields – these are the bread-and-butter pre-occupations of site management teams. Staying on top of this catalogue requires staff capacity and underpinning finance. Whether in 1 school or 20 in a trust, these aspects matter in creating the proper environment within which people flourish.

Sadly, there is too often a careless attitude towards tree maintenance, flower beds, courtyard areas and even entrance plant pots – these matter too. A number of schools have a rota of governors to walk the site once a fortnight and report back to the executive. Those boards which rigorously practice this are making a statement about environmental wellbeing, which in turn makes students and staff alike proud to attend the school.

Walk or drive into the school where you are a governor. Try to see it with fresh eyes. What *are* your first impressions of the maintenance of flower borders, of helpful signage, of space for bicycles, of access for wheelchairs, of ease of finding the right buzzer?

## C   MONEY

Completing the triumvirate are the trials and tribulations of those who manage budgets. Fortunately in most schools and trusts there are business managers and chief operating officers who, at different scale, manage highly competent teams. Succession planning is something for a board to keep an eye on; often a leading accountant in the team either retires, is poached or moves out of the area, and a few months of struggle and make-do ensue.

Most boards manage to attract at least one or two members who can glance at a financial spreadsheet, sniff the air and ask probing questions of the accounting officer. Indeed, it is regularly observable just how many retired accountants enjoy a day a fortnight as a governor working alongside the finance team – and are very much welcomed as long as they remember the strategic/operational divide.

To observe the business manager and 'finance' governor sparring and nearly always coming to the same positive conclusions frequently provides light entertainment to those governors who are delighted someone else *really* grasps the figures.

What is critical for all boards is transparency with the bottom line, with financial projections rooted in accurate staff costs and secure student number projections. The prevailing theme of 'no surprises' is nowhere more important in good governance than in the balance sheet.

****

## THE LAW OF THE LAND

If you happen to sit on a board that includes a lawyer, even better a judge, you will have on hand someone who will explain the niceties of the law, usually in beautifully formed and precise phrases. If they do not have the answer to a question arising, they surely know where to look up the answer. And that can be very reassuring to governors and trustees, without having recourse to an external and probably costly opinion.

Good clerks are worth their weight in gold in this domain, able to explain the niceties of freedom of information requests (FoIs) or subject access reports (SARs) – the flurry of initialisms and acronyms starts. And where complaints procedures need to be followed, they must be followed scrupulously, taking advice as appropriate. CEOs and chairs are in the main good at this.

Compliance matters, and matters very much. Whether in the domain of cyber-security, lockdown procedures, authentication of qualifications, contracts with builders, boarding house medicine cupboards – from the macro to the micro there must be collective executive/board vigilance, precision and clarity.

One chair opens each board meeting with this question to the headteacher: 'So what's keeping you awake at night?' The fact that it is routine is enjoyed by everyone attending and often prompts governors to share their own answers; the seriousness beneath the question informs board thinking about risk.

More widely in the system, whether in special, primary or secondary, experience indicates that executives and boards move together effectively in relation to risk assessment. There is that happy combination of insights and oversight providing a restless, never complacent approach.

# ASIDE

## WHAT TO DO?

A headteacher makes various internal changes to the processes around references that the school provides for sixth form students. One of the sixth form staff disagrees with the changes.

At the next board meeting a governor brings up the issue of references for sixth form students and questions the new changes that have been made.

*What should the chair do in this situation?. . .*

****

Five students are engaged in illegal behaviour involving illicit substances. School leaders find evidence of incidents that happened outside of school. The behaviour and conduct of these five students is seriously impinging on other students, and rumours in the school community are quickly gathering momentum.

The headteacher, after consulting the chair and key governors, acts on the external evidence and expels the students. The parents of some of the expelled students then engage lawyers and the school becomes embroiled in a protracted and expensive legal situation.

Given the serious damage to the school's reputation, was it the right call to expel the students?

*The governing board meets to discuss. . .*

****

# SENECA

**The accomplished board is comfortable in its own skin.**

What kind of governing body or trust board do you want to be, when observed from the outside?

As a regular reviewer of schools in the UK and internationally, probably my two best received compliments to teachers and leaders at the end of a visit are:

- This is a delightful environment in which to be a child.
- This is a school at ease with itself.

Applied to governance, one might affirm: this is a board where it is a pleasure to be a member, and a board which feels at ease with itself.

For this author there are two crunch questions when it comes to leadership in any context, to which the last paragraph of this chapter returns:

- What's worth fighting for in leadership?
- Why should anyone be led by you?

Much of what is said about the qualities you need to be a leader – principal or chair of governors – is hardly new and has often been said much more succinctly and elegantly over the course of human history. It is mostly all there somewhere: in the works of philosophers such as Plato, Aristotle, Machiavelli and Burke; in good history books, and in novels.

The contemporary world has a remarkable capacity for thinking that its ideas are wholly novel. In that spirit, this chapter takes the work of one of the Greek philosophers Seneca, to hold the mirror up to a board of governors. If Seneca does not work for you, try another set of ideas, ancient or modern, that do reflect what kind of governing body you want to be.

Seneca moved in the highest political circles of Rome in the 1st century CE. He was a self-proclaimed follower of Stoicism. Seneca's works are the oldest complete writings that survive by a Stoic, its beliefs and practices originally founded in Athens around 300 BCE. For Seneca, philosophy was a source of guidance about how to live. His reflections – taught and studied down the ages – deal with highly practical issues as relevant today as they were when first written.

What are the ideas that have stood the test of centuries? Put simply, there are seven which a governing board might think about when it considers its ways of doing, being and how others think of it.

## Keep calm

Contemporary parlance on badges has added 'and carry on'. Seneca argued that nothing is more destructive than violent emotion out of control. Emotions like anger, jealousy and fear of others undermine good human relationships. He advocated tolerance, recognising we are humans born to err.

## Avoid constant distraction

The contention here is that we are too readily distracted by trivialities in our daily lives, and that it becomes impossible to do anything well if we are trying to do too many things at once. To anyone who complains that life is too short, his retort is too much of it gets wasted by trivia.

## Prioritise leisure

The argument in this section is that it is important to have a whole series of interesting activities outside of paid work. It is vital to slow down, to be fully awake in the moment. Time needs to be found for quiet and rational reflection about the world and our place within it.

## Live modestly

Seneca observed that too many people waste a large part of their life in pursuit of wealth they will never have time to enjoy. He argues for being content with what one has, not continuing to chase after diversions and illusory riches.

## Learn from challenges

This aspect of his thinking focused on the view that it is only through experiencing bad luck that people get the chance to develop their characters. Stoic ethics say that the only thing that is genuinely good is an excellent, virtuous character. In today's world, the phrase might well be: what does not kill us makes us stronger.

## Do not be too ambitious

Linked to above, the need to learn from setbacks. Ambition can fuel our desires and expectations, which in turn lead to frustrations and disappointment. Resilience in the contemporary workplace might be one interpretation.

## Find a meaningful activity

It is important for a good life to have a meaningful activity, no matter what it is. Find something that, however long your life, you look back at it with a sense of something achieved, something which benefitted you and others.

In essence, Seneca presents living a happy life as relatively easy. It is the hyper-busy, constantly distracted, emotionally invested, over ambitious life that is hard work.

## WHAT'S WORTH FIGHTING FOR? WHY SHOULD ANYONE BE LED BY YOU?

To return to the opening of this chapter. How does your board operate? How is it viewed?

The distinguished French artist Paul Cezanne painted and drew Mt St Victoire in Provence over 100 times, never satisfied with the outcome and saying that mastery eluded him. The great governing boards I come across have in their command most or all of the constituent features covered in this A–Z. They are not perfect, nor do they see themselves as the finished item.

What distinguishes them is their steely determination to deliver what they have said they will deliver, over time, and they are not prepared to deviate from those goals. They do not have the arrogance of certainty, yet the members are united in the ambition to provide the best all-round education for the children and young people they serve. That may be 80 in a special school, 300 in a primary, 1200 in a secondary or 10,000 across a trust.

Furthermore, there is a quiet inward confidence shared between members and the executive. The community and linked stakeholders know the school or trust are in capable hands; when governors write to families it is a communication which may raise proper questions, but it can be trusted. There is from teachers and students a firm belief that they are being led in this important enterprise by informed volunteers who have their interests at heart.

There is a double couplet which concludes *A Hard Rain's a-Gonna Fall*, the famous anthem by Bob Dylan:

> And I'll tell it and think it and speak it and breathe it
>
> And reflect it from the mountain so all souls can see it
>
> Then I'll stand on the ocean until I start sinkin'
>
> But I'll know my song well before I start singin'

There is about great governance that common purpose of mission, that knowledge of what is to be delivered, that strong sense of being proud ambassadors who know their song well.

# ASIDE

## WHAT TO DO?

Two students share nude photos of another student who it transpires threatened to take their own life as a result of the sharing of the nude photos. The principal acts immediately and involves the local authorities, including the police. The two students who shared the photos are asked to leave the school.

Lawyers are involved as one set of parents believes the school has overstepped its authority in searching their child's mobile phone without their express permission – despite the parents, during the admissions process, digitally agreeing to adhere to the school's policies.

With incidents involving social media and child protection increasing, and the use of lawyers by parents becoming more commonplace, what is the right level of involvement of governors in school matters and the school's application of its policies?

*The governing body hold a special meeting on the subject...*

****

A staff governor on a trust local governing body has recently been elected as a local councillor and sides with some local opposition to academisation. The local chair talks about this to the principal and the CEO, but no action follows.

The chair feels strongly that this situation is untenable. Further discussions with the CEO and principal reveal real tensions. The local chair decides this must be dealt with by the trust board and refers it to the trust chair for action.

*The trust board meets to consider...*

****

# TRAINING

**Time is well spent training a board to be the best it can be.**

The following were presented over a couple of years to the principal of an international school, not particularly difficult decisions for someone experienced. Nonetheless he shared them with his board chair on each occasion as it took them back to first principles.

What would your decisions and actions have been?

- Deciding to what extent a non-religious school is also a secular space: for example, do we let school premises to religious groups associated with the school community, and what is our view on signs of religious affiliation as part of staff dress?

- Responding to a Chinese diplomat parent who objected to a representative of the Dalai Lama being invited to speak to students and/or demanded a right of reply.

- Dealing with a parental complaint about the choice of a novel by Salman Rushdie for study by younger students.

- Reacting to a parent's criticism that an article on education for human rights in one of our school community magazines talked about the debt that the world owed, over the last 300 years, to England and France for their development of 'the idea of human rights' but failed to mention these countries' colonial legacies.

- Deciding whether to continue to get students to support a humanitarian charity that distributes aid to children having found out that one of its subsidiary objectives, in a different part of its activity, was Christian evangelisation.

- Responding to a member of staff who objected to the commemoration of World Holocaust Day as something imposed from above by 'the pressures of the day' rather than as something arising spontaneously from within the school as they felt it should have been.

Arguably, no amount of training prepares leaders for these kinds of decisions. One learns by doing, by failing wisely, by reflecting over time on the constituent features of good decision making.

## ON THE JOB TRAINING

Devotees of the '10,000 hours of purposeful practice' camp (a concept originally researched by psychologist Anders Ericsson and popularised by Malcolm Gladwell), would argue that there is simply no substitute for putting in the hours if you want to master something. Chefs, Grand Prix drivers, roofers, gardeners and dentists at the top of their game have all paid their dues.

Teachers teach about 1,000 hours a year, so on that basis they are performing pretty well after a decade. Governors might reflect on their own trades, crafts and professions – how long did it take to be really proficient, and are you still improving? Sports folk often quote the celebrated golfer who, when asked about his run of victories and the role of luck, observed: 'the more I practise the luckier I get'.

There may well be a few headteachers, governors and trustees in the country who have sat through close on 10,000 hours of board meetings. If you have, as the French say: 'chapeau!'

Participating in committee and board meetings, pre-meetings, school visits, interviews and the panoply of pleasurable engagements that a long-serving governor will have experienced must surely add up to the best kind of training one can have. Certainly, if one reflects on those experiences, draws key lessons from them, and seeks to be an ever more accomplished governor, then perhaps one's training is complete.

# IN-SERVICE TRAINING

The quality of in-service training for teachers and leaders has improved immeasurably in recent years; at its best it is bespoke to needs, time limited and focused upon the immediate requirements teachers have identified.

The same is true for governors. We all have to start somewhere. Induction to a new board is generally well handled by the chair and clerk, bringing new members up to speed on the essence of an organisation, perhaps through the staff handbook, and certainly running a few sessions on the key local and national documents (e.g. Keeping children safe in education 2024, DfE) which all governors must be familiar with.

There are occasions in the lifetime of a group of governors when there has been a difficult incident in the wider community, not necessarily in the school. This might result in the chair inviting an external voice to explain what has happened and perhaps what the reverberations might be within the school for a period. Those external inputs, as needs arise, are invaluable.

Legislation does not stand still and the 'next risk on the horizon' beckons. It could be cyber-security, it could be financial scamming, it could be new regulations on the sports fields. Yes, the executive will lead but having at least one governor available to stay abreast of a particular subject is ever welcome as part of the oversight duties. The clerk will usually keep a good record of what training governors have done – and prompt with a smile where needed.

Local authorities and trusts regularly identify through questionnaires and surveys what governors' and trustees' topical training requirements are, and seek to meet those needs, mindful that volunteer time is at a premium. Many local authorities hold seminars and conferences, at their best led by directors of education who know that listening to the voices of board members is a vital part of the feedback loop when heading up a multi-million pound service.

Importantly, the National Governors Association and the Confederation of School Trusts are highly respected friends within the system, providing a wealth of up-to-date information and great training opportunities:

- National Governors Association: https://www.nga.org.uk/
- Confederation of School Trusts: https://cstuk.org.uk/

Strategy sessions (away-days or similar) have their place, perhaps on an annual basis, and especially in trusts where it is an occasion to gather all headteachers and chairs together to review the year past, plan for the year ahead and make important recommendations to the trust board about, for example, whether the trust should consolidate or expand. Many trusts across the country these days are leading employers within their county, and inviting county chief executives to talk at such annual gatherings is invaluable.

Can training prepare for every eventuality? No. What it can do is complement your experiences in meetings, in visits to your school, in talking with fellow governors. There is a climate in just about every school today that values governors, and leaders will do all in their reach to enhance good governance with the right training and development opportunities.

## A CONFIDENTIAL WORD

Not every induction course covers this topic as well as it might. It is a topic that should permeate all training.

A make-or-break aspect of a board's own internal rules is the question of confidentiality. Every governor, from their own experiences beyond the school, will know this to be true. It is paramount to get this right, no stone unturned. Confidentiality – and judgements about what is confidential and what is not – is rooted in mutual trust amongst a group of people who have access to 'restricted' information. The dictionary definition of 'confidential' – 'intended to be kept secret' – is not necessarily helpful.

One person's definition of confidentiality can truly be: 'I tell one person at a time.' It is worth reflecting that Nolan's elegant seven principles of public life (pages 88–90) do not include confidentiality, opting for other vocabulary to cover similar territory. Yet all parties trying to agree what they mean by the word is vital for trusted governance.

When there is a confidential item for consideration at a meeting it is often helpfully presented on a different colour paper, and/or as a separate online file. (In this context it is also useful if the chair explains where FoI requests can lead.) That confidential item – regularly these focus on people: young people and safeguarding; adults and employment matters – will be duly considered by the board and appropriate minutes taken. It is rare for anyone in this context to break confidences.

It is in other committee and board meetings where the word 'confidential' can arise casually, gain momentum under a particular item, leading the chair to say 'let's be mindful of confidentiality here'. It is in these 'casual' cases where after an in-person or virtual meeting – to use the old war phrase – 'careless talk costs lives'. One person's take on confidentiality can be another's interpretation of transparency.

This is never easy territory for governors, especially when the next day they are at the school gate or helping with a school visit or are friends with a person whose name has been mentioned at a meeting. We must strive as volunteers to be as respectful as we can of others' privacy, especially if we have had access to private information. We must pay special attention to how we use the word 'confidential', *carefully* not carelessly.

As governors – as in the best traditions of HMI – we should seek 'to do good as we go'.

---

# ASIDE

## WHAT TO DO?

An academy trust is struggling to fill vacancies on its board. A new chief executive takes steps to regularise the way the trust is run but this leads to staff unrest. The trust board decide the chief executive should leave.

Previous trustees who appointed the chief executive have now become Members of the trust and are furious at not being involved in this decision.

*The trustees and members agree to meet. . .*

****

A trust chief executive appoints her sister as chief finance officer on a lower than usual salary and tells the board the trust cannot afford to appoint someone externally at usual market rates.

The DfE, through the regional director, ask the board to discuss their recruitment arrangements and report back.

*The matter is on the agenda at the next board meeting. . .*

****

# UNCONVENTIONAL

**Valuing the unorthodox and the maverick is critical to fine governance.**

Life can often deal out some extraordinary slaps in the face. When it happens to us we can feel very indignant, depressed or got at, especially if someone is unkind enough to say 'serves you right'. Of course, when the tables are turned we sometimes find it difficult to stop laughing at other people's misfortunes.

Here are a handful of true global stories, recorded month by month, from one year's news:

*January*

*Police*, the journal of the boys in blue, reported that a suspicious-looking cardboard box has been found outside a Territorial Army centre in Bristol. The TA called the police, who called an army bomb disposal unit, which blew the box up – to discover it was full of leaflets on how to deal with suspicious-looking packages.

*March*

Neighbours ignored a blaze at the Bermondsey studios where the television series *London's Burning* is being filmed – they thought the conflagration was part of the show. When fire crews arrived at the four-storey building to tackle the outbreak, the same residents complained about the noise.

*June*

After 326 days underground, a 73-year-old miner emerged from a pit in Colorado, thinking that he had achieved a new best for the Guinness Book of Records, only to be told that the record was, in fact, 463 days.

*September*

John Cook returned home to Nelson, New Zealand, from a holiday in the US to find that his wooden five-bedroom house had been stolen, not a trace of it anywhere.

*December*

Three hundred tons of sand put down to make a new bathing beach at Burnham-on-Crouch, Essex, disappeared when the tide went out.

The unconventional makes us reflect on the conventional. In a risk-averse society we are fearful of taking even measured risks. We look over our shoulders to check we are 'in line'. Does that blind us sometimes to doing things differently, to challenging orthodoxies, to marginalising those who would make us think differently?

When the wind of change blows, does your board build walls, or windmills?

School and trust governance is dominated by the conventional, by following rules and regulations. Given the important responsibilities boards have towards students and staff, that is as it should be. Yet we need to make space for the mavericks and the unorthodox for they often bring a cutting-edge, a tad of humour and light-heartedness, and alternative ways of thinking which enrich decision making. The best governing bodies make space for such approaches.

Here are a few to consider, accept or reject – your call!

- In Chairs (page 15), Graham Taylor jokingly said that he liked his chair (Elton John) because he was wealthy, busy and lived a long way away. Or read about Robert Palmer (page 5) and his working relationship with the author. What does the principal of your school most value about the chair – their absence or their presence?

- You have a very busy board member who travels widely for his business. He is trilingual, has a great address book, speaks little at meetings but when he speaks he is invariably worth listening to. He quotes the maxim that '80% of success is turning up' – and that is accurate, he attends just about four main board meetings in five and has no time for committees. Should the chair ask him to stand down?

- Another member of the board is an inveterate latecomer, always with a seemingly plausible excuse as he slips into meetings. He recounts the story that it is a habit he developed at school, telling the teacher wondrous tales: 'I found a bird lying on the side of the road, so took it to the vet, that's why I'm late.' We all recognise the type. What should the chair do about this one? Forgive and forgive, and pray for him?

- You have a governor who is constantly harking on about how 'they do it better at the other secondary school in town'. Do you suggest nicely that he joins the other school's governing body? Do you say that 'the grass is greener until you have mown it a few times'? To borrow the words of US President Lyndon Johnson, is it better to have him inside the tent peeing out, or outside the tent peeing in?

- 'To vote or not to vote' in board meetings. Some folk like voting. Others, in the Quaker tradition, favour affirming and not raising hands. My own strong preference is the latter. Votes divide volunteers, and folk can leave meetings feeling they have been defeated. What does your board do?

- One of your board members is a marketing guru. He constantly quotes the elevator pitch, those compelling few words on any subject – see pages 173–174 for a summary of this book. Furthermore, he argues powerfully that no presentation should be longer than three slides, or on one side of A4, font 12. Does the board adopt his guide as their preferred house style? What do the executive think?

- In the same spirit, the chair has a mantra to the executive and certainly to any adviser who turns up to the board meeting: 'Be brief, be bold, be gone.' Good advice when time is tight, or too limiting?

- Your chair does not allow AOB at the end of a meeting. Items will not be discussed without prior notice and relevant papers. She does favour the final item being 'Unintended Consequences': five minutes reflection around the table on things that have been decided during a meeting which may resonate inconveniently in the future. Unconventional, yet worth trying?

- And, finally, there is the poet in your midst who reminds even the finance folk that in her culture of romanticism, '2 + 2 = $4\frac{1}{2}$, and that's good enough.' Is she right sometimes?

## SHOUT-OUT

Where altruism and self-interest collide, you have a deal. Where the conventional and the unconventional co-exist, you have sparkling conversations and – adroitly handled – enhanced governance.

It may not be a characteristic of being British but we need to learn not to be shy about championing successes. The unconventional must triumph here.

The poet Rudyard Kipling wrote of 'triumph and disaster' (Kipling, 1910) being two imposters that need similar treatment. A school with 500 children and 50 staff has 550 daily opportunities to see 'triumphs and disasters'. Whilst dealing carefully with the latter, we need to champion achievements, to shout-out the good and the great in our schools.

Board members should bring objectivity to decision making yet can surely allow themselves to be subjective in their ambassadorial role. There may be in any one term the following which need appropriate congratulations and publicity.

- Cup-winning performances in the hockey and badminton teams
- 100% attendance for 100 pupils
- A highly complimentary inspection of the special school boarding house
- The headteacher nominated by their peers nationally for outstanding contributions to primary education
- The hosting of a high-profile industrialist to congratulate the design and technology department.

****

Perhaps written into every governor and trustee handbook should be these words from the poet E.E. Cummings, asserting in *A Poet's Advice to Students* (Cummings, 1955):

> To be nobody but yourself in a world which is doing its best, night and day, to make you somebody else – means to fight the hardest battle which any human being can fight; and never stop fighting.

---

# ASIDE

## WHAT TO DO?

A governing body agree that their headteacher will become executive head over their school and a nearby school which has just had a poor external review.

A parent governor missed the meeting where this was agreed and asks at the next meeting for the decision to be reversed. The head has already taken up the new role – and is enjoying it.

The chair refuses that the matter be discussed again. The parent governor inspires a parental petition asking that the school have the head to themselves.

*The governing body holds an emergency meeting...*

****

At a time when the news in the mass media is often about a conflict between two countries in another part of the world, a member of teaching staff writes an article in a widely read local newspaper supporting one side in the conflict.

At the following board meeting a trustee known to be closely connected with the other side in the conflict objects strongly to the teacher's action and asks for him to be disciplined and not to repeat this action.

*How do the governors respond?...*

****

---

# VOLUNTEERS

## Motivating a group of volunteers 'to turn up next time' should not be underplayed.

This is the true joy in life, being used for a purpose recognised by yourself as a mighty one. Being a force of nature instead of a feverish, selfish little clod of ailments and grievances, complaining that the world will not devote itself to making you happy. I am of the opinion that my life belongs to the whole community and as long as I live, it is my privilege to do for it what I can. I want to be thoroughly used up when I die, for the harder I work, the more I live. I rejoice in life for its own sake. Life is no brief candle to me. It is a sort of splendid torch which I have got hold of for the moment and I want to make it burn as brightly as possible before handing it on to future generations.

(Shaw, 1903)

George Bernard Shaw lived to the age of 94. In his lifetime he wrote more than 60 plays and was a prolific polemicist in print until his death in 1950. He lived up to his own dictum.

Shaw writes of his life belonging to the whole community. Volunteering lies at the heart of what it is to be human, where altruism is as important as self-interest – indeed, where does one end and the other begin?

We start volunteering often from the earliest of ages, and schools are awash with students offering their services in so many different settings. As adults we may be drawn to a particular cause through politics, local social issues or through family experiences.

People with children at a local school offer their time to read or accompany school visits and then often get drawn into parent–teacher associations and then into governance. The routes are many. The outcomes the same: finding oneself engaged, involved and committed to serving on a board.

Yet there comes a point in time when the following happens to most of us in our volunteering lifetimes. You have been on a board for four years and you are finding the time commitment difficult to sustain. You have missed a couple of meetings in succession and are feeling guilty about it. Should you continue or do the honest thing and tell the chair your time is up? Your period of office has another year plus to run. You just cannot decide.

**Five questions to weigh**

**1. What is giving you greatest satisfaction as a governor?**

What drew you into governance, namely to serve the local community and see first-hand what young people are engaged with in the 21st century, still holds you. Reading weekly newsletters which feature curriculum developments you have helped shape, attending awards evenings, welcoming special guests to the school – these are not to be taken for granted.

You enjoy being associated with the school and enjoy the opportunity in the high street to meet parents and be a proud ambassador. You especially enjoy being on the curriculum and assessment committee linked to your own employment at one of the examination boards. And whilst the board meetings are time-consuming and often clash with work commitments, you enjoy the company and interactions with fellow governors.

**2. How do you know if you are having an impact?**

Coming to the end of your fourth year you can see the impact of some of the decisions you were party to when you first joined. The introduction of a reading and phonics scheme across Year 7, which you urged, has had a measurable impact on the number of pupils improving their reading ages by the end of Year 9. Recommendations from your committee to the main board about re-imagining the personal, social and health programme were taken up a year ago; recent conversations with senior students are a testament to how well the new programme has been received.

And you have much enjoyed the times when you have been part of an interviewing panel for new teachers, especially for your own subject, maths – teachers of mathematics seem an increasingly rare breed.

### 3. What do my fellow governors think of my contributions?

You know from conversations outside as well as inside meetings that fellow governors see you as a very good listener; they know equally that when you contribute in debate, your views are well worth listening to.

You worry that missing a couple of meetings will mean others will think less well of you. On reflection, there have been a number of fellow governors who for one reason or another have missed meetings. Maybe one has to accept that, as long as it does not become habitual?

### 4. What could the chair and executive do to keep you turning up?

That's a difficult one. We receive excellent papers in good time prior to meetings; we meet in agreeable surroundings, with appealing refreshments. The senior leadership team members who attend the meetings are well briefed and good listeners. The chair includes me in discussions in their characteristically warm style and is genuinely open to challenge. Importantly, we finish meetings on time and with a clear minuting of what the action points are before we meet again.

Communication is excellent. The chair invariably writes a short thank you to the board after each meeting, and co-writes a note with the headteacher to explain to staff the key matters we have covered. We practise the values of the school as a people business.

### 5. When will you know it is time to leave?

You see parent governors coming to the end of their period of office and some naturally step away. Some are asked to stay on in a different capacity; some governors have their period of office extended. There is not a lot of churn on the board yet sufficient to have fresh thinking join, certainly in the five years you have been a governor. New members reinvigorate both the committees and the main board.

You will make a break when you feel, deep-down, that in the nicest possible way you have made yourself redundant – i.e. you feel you have given as much time and commitment and good thinking to the board as you can, and it is now a moment to pass on the torch. You will be missed but you can choose, or not, to continue attending school events. You live in the community so you will stay loosely in touch. As the adage on the coffee mug given to retiring teachers reads: old teachers never die, they just lose their class.

It's a personal decision and one which it is well worth talking through with a trusted fellow governor and/or the chair. The important thing is: if you leave, do not give a backwards glance with regret.

✳✳✳✳

The above is reflecting the scenario of an individual school governor. The same considerations will be true if you are a trustee. There may be additional ones relating to travel times to meetings if you are not local; changed work or family commitments; you were a founding trustee and you feel it is time for fresh ideas; the CEO is about to leave, you helped appoint the successor, and now think that new CEO should have the opportunity to bring on new trustees.

One reads regularly of people in their nineties who continue to deliver meals on wheels, staff phonelines for Samaritans, tour with the mobile library, help at the hospital as guides, read weekly with primary children – the volunteering bug does not leave them. They are determined, in Shaw's words, to be 'thoroughly used up'. Society salutes them.

# ASIDE

## WHAT TO DO?

One of the two staff representatives on the board raises a question during a meeting about an email that has been sent by a member of the school's management team to a teacher, complaining that the words used in the email were racist.

The staff representative also mentions that it has been drawn to the head's attention and that the head has not taken any action in response to it.

In responding to the question, the chair says that she has already heard of the complaint from the staff representative. The head is completely unaware of the issue and has not been approached about it prior to the meeting, either by the staff representative or by the chair.

*What follows?. . .*

\*\*\*\*

A prominent tobacco company, many of whose employees have children at a private international school, has offered a substantial donation that would help the school to build a centre for children with special educational needs.

To date, these children have only been partially integrated into the school's mainstream classes, and would benefit greatly from being part of the school community and participating in whole-school activities.

The head and finance director support acceptance of the offer but trustees have informed the chair of their opposition.

*How does the chair manage the upcoming board meeting in which this item is on the agenda?. . .*

\*\*\*\*

# WALKABOUT

**Engaged boards make time to walk around the 'estate' of the organisation.**

The word 'walkabout' is often associated with the rite of passage of young Aboriginal people, exploring their natural landscape. In James Vance Marshall's novel *Walkabout* (Vance, 1959) he memorably describes the coming together of the two white children, lost in the desert after a plane crash, and the indigenous 'bush boy':

> The three children stood looking at each other in the middle of the Australian desert. Motionless as the outcrops of granite they stared, and stared, and stared. Between them the distance was less than the spread of an outstretched arm, but more than a hundred thousand years.

No spoilers...in the novel it is the bush boy's detailed knowledge of his vast estate that enables the lost children to survive.

For governors and trustees, the more detailed knowledge they have of the 'estate' for which they are responsible, then the likelihood is that decisions in meetings rooms will be better informed. Avoiding a step into the operational, it really is very important to know what life is like on the corridors and in classrooms and on playing fields.

## PROTOCOLS

This is an important place to start. Securing a common agreement with the board on the purpose of any visit is the starting point of trust and a fruitful visit. It is important to remember that visits are a snapshot in time, and judgements should not be made arbitrarily.

Pages 185–187 in Section Two outline one school's very thorough protocol, well worth dipping into. Every school should have something similar, to avoid any subsequent misunderstandings. It includes what a visit is *not* about:

- Inspection
- Making judgements about the professional expertise of the teacher
- Checking on your own children
- Pursuing a personal agenda
- Arriving with inflexible pre-conceived ideas
- Governors need to be mindful of confidentiality issues and will not discuss the visits outside the governing body.

## WHAT AM I FINDING?

Quite common practice in many schools today is combining a 'walkabout' with the termly board meeting:

| | |
|---|---|
| 8.30am | Arrival and watch pupils arrive, go to library, breakfast club, etc. |
| 9am | Short briefing by headteacher on focus of 'walkabout'. |
| 9.15am | Visit areas of the school in pairs, accompanied by a member of staff. |
| 10.15am | Reconvene over coffee and discuss what governors have seen. |
| 10.45am-1pm | Board meeting. |

The success of the visits lies in the headteacher's briefing and what, on this particular day, governors are asked to focus on and thus be able to comment upon. The same topic may deliberately be on the board agenda – wise planning!

This day's visit may be looking in classrooms at a new phonics programme or a revised personal and social health course, or a visit to Year 11 classes to look at how examination revision is being addressed. Senior teams welcome an external eye: what are you seeing that we have missed?

A school might be having a special look at what students are saying about lessons, about how they are taught and how they learn. In which case, thoughtfully orchestrated, pairs of governors can meet small groups of students from different year groups, with a short set of questions.

Students need to have it explained to them the purpose of the meetings and be encouraged to speak up, to speak with their eyes – and to speak their minds. This is all about improving the great double act in schools, which is learning and teaching.

What is happening from the student's viewpoint?

- Am I happy and motivated in class, collaborating with my friends to make progress?
- Am I using my time well in class?
- Is the teacher aiding and extending me, given my starting points?
- Does the teacher deepen my learning from time to time?

In fact these are the kind of questions parents might ask of their children over the kitchen table, so governors asking these questions in a gentle spirit of enquiry is good practice.

Whenever I am party to such conversations between governors and pupils, I never stop marvelling at how perceptive students are. You do not need inspectors in schools to tell headteachers the strengths and weaknesses of classrooms – just ask the students, regularly, and enter into open discussions with them about next best steps, for both teachers and pupils.

Invariably, governors come back together keen to share what they have heard, and more often than not expressing their thanks for the privilege of hearing young voices. From a governor's point of view, there is surprise in the precision of what students say, or in just how articulate and mature they are. There is invariably pride expressed in being associated with the school.

Governors, and indeed leaders at all levels in schools, do not interview students often enough about learning; it is too easy to talk about school dinners and after-school clubs, important though these are.

# FEEDBACK AND FEEDFORWARD

## Governors

Moving beyond the case study above where walkabouts start each governors' meeting, it is common practice for schools to have an annual programme of visits set out for board members. Beyond the common protocols outlined above, critical to the success and credibility over time of these are:

- Teachers see the purpose of the visits: this may involve a subject-linked governor who has established a mutually enjoyable link with a curriculum area.
- Governors see the purpose of the visits: what am I as a layperson bringing to the party?
- Everyone understands what the outcome will be: short verbal feedback, a 300-word written feedback within three days or an oral feedforward at the next curriculum committee – which is it to be?

It is certainly recommended practice that once a year the executive and board review their programme of visits, to tweak arrangements and be sharp about the value added. Teachers enjoy showing off their practice, yet it is an interruption to the diurnal round. Visits are time consuming for volunteers; some board members may be free during the day and can take on more, others may find the timings difficult. There is understanding and respect for one another's diaries.

## Trustees

Trustees may have a wider canvas to work with, being responsible for a group of primaries in a town trust or for a mix of schools across two counties. The location of the schools will shape how often schools can expect a visit from board members, yet it is vital that trustees see schools in action: to get a sense of the quality of education; to look carefully at the state of the buildings; and to talk to teachers and support staff about what they are proud of and what resources they might be short of.

Much depends on the geographical spread of the trust.

Board chairs need to take a lead with the CEO to arrange a schedule of visits which if not necessarily including every school every year does ensure that trustees have made some visits so they can speak with authority at meetings. Mistrust from principals sets in when they think 'them at HQ' do not understand their contexts. Principals want to know that when a report on their school is being presented to the main board it is being read by at least a couple of members who are familiar first-hand with their context.

It is not uncommon in trusts for some trustees to chair individual school boards; that way lies an insider knowledge which is (a) valued by headteachers and staff and (b) warmly applauded and appreciated by fellow trustees.

Rereading the stories of Sir Ken Morrison (page 3) pacing the shopping aisles of his stores is a reminder that there is no substitute for the in-person walkabout.

---

# ASIDE

## WHAT TO DO?

A local authority junior school shares a site with one of its local authority feeder infant schools. The buildings are 10m apart. The governing bodies of the two schools – and their headteachers – agree that families would be better served if they combined to form a single school.

The governing bodies approach the local authority, which gives support and encouragement in the background and facilitates a public consultation. The outcome is overwhelmingly supportive of the plan.

The local authority then informs the governing bodies that it will not permit the merger, leaving them to deal with communicating to families.

*What do governors do regarding immediate communication and longer term plans?. . .*

\*\*\*\*

---

A small primary school serving a deprived area is part of a five-school academy trust dominated by two very large secondary schools. Following inspection, the primary school is rated good by Ofsted. The inspection report is glowing in its comments about trust support.

However, the school governing body takes a very different view, being of the opinion that the trust chair talks a good game whilst the trust board, and its CEO, ignore the needs of the school and any reports or requests from its governing body.

The governing body takes the view that the school's success is in spite of, rather than because of, the trust and that further development of the school is being impeded. Attempts by the governing body to bring about change at trust level do not bear fruit.

*What could or should the governing body do?...*

****

# XENACIOUS

## Scanning the horizon for 'what next' distinguishes excellent governance.

*'Xenacious' – 'filled with a yearning for change or growth'*

It was the celebrated sci-fi author William Gibson who cannily observed that the future is already here, but it's just not very evenly distributed. The extraordinary becomes the commonplace, at a faster and faster rate. Like the frog which slowly boils in the pan, realising too late that it is cooked, inertia in education can limit agile adjustments to changing circumstances.

Scanning the education horizon, what does this author see ahead? We are in the dying years of the current DfE.

In my book *The Restless School* (Blatchford, 2014), I wrote:

> Walk into the foyer of the Department for Education in London, and there are photos of all the Secretaries of State for Education since Rab Butler and Ellen Wilkinson in the 1940s; what most of them have in common is their fewer than three-years tenure of office. Many distinguished and fine public servants among them, long-term planning is not in the nature of the office.

> In my school journey years, the current DfE has also been called: the Ministry of Education; Department of Education and Science; Department for Education; Department for Education and Employment; Department for Education and Skills; and Department for Children, Schools and Families. I do not guess here what other acronyms may befall it, prior to its complete abolition sometime in the late 2020s.

What are we looking at here? Certainly, since the hyper-active days of Michael Gove as Secretary of State (2010-14), the DfE has drifted aimlessly under ten different leaders, the longest serving of whom was Gavin Williamson at two years, one month and 22 days.

There are three credible scenarios for the ending of the DfE in its present guise.

*First: departments of state will merge*

A new era in central government departments is upon us, shaped by the urgent need to fund the defence of the land. Government has recently disclosed 'billions lavished on projects abroad', including £500,000 to supply electric cars to Albanian prisons.

The litany in similar vein is a matter of public record. The Home Office has found evidence of 'excessive spending on contracts handed out to external suppliers'. Ministers at the MOD noted 'no clear accountability' and 'added complexity where simplicity is needed…no wonder it took an average of six years for a large programme to get underway'.

So which department of state subsumes education?

*Second: the mayors will run education*

The current deputy prime minister, Angela Rayner, is determined to deliver on devolution and local government reorganisation. The arguments are again about cost-savings – and moving power down to the local level.

Who would bet against Andy Burnham in Manchester, Ben Houchen in Tees Valley or Andrea Jenkyns the mayor of Lincolnshire running education more efficiently and 'closer to the people'?

*Third: the Department for Young People arrives*

With devolution enacted, an advanced multi-academy trust landscape, AI in its pomp, and ever more financial pressures, there may still be a need for some slimmed-down co-ordination at the centre.

Let us propose a Department for Young People (DYP), focused on health, learning and opportunities for the coming generation. The latest figures of close to one million NEETs are a scar, as is the continued neglect of the 'forgotten third'.

The future of government departments will be measured in their agility and clarity; their demonstrable value for money; their flexibility to respond to very rapid change in society; most of all, their ability to work within a dynamic political landscape of coalition partners. The bureaucratic state must be reimagined.

****

## SCANNING: WHAT IS THE SCHOOL/TRUST VERY GOOD AT?

Perhaps on your annual strategy day, with time to reflect and to blow your own trumpets, what would you brainstorm and say your school or trust is very good at? What are you especially proud of that has potential for development, for sharing beyond your own boundaries?

Which of these might it be?

1.  The quality of early years provision which you would like to expand into a wider 'children's centre' offer.

2.  The speech and language centre that you host on site for the local authority which is ripe for expansion given identified need from other schools.

3.  The extensive outdoor learning provision – including a mini-farm – which could be opened up for wider community use.

4.  The recently completed music and arts buildings which cry out for partnership with the town.

5.  The now popular sixth-form centre which could be federated with a couple of other sixth forms in the area, thereby creating an outstanding hub for the education of 16–19-year-olds in the city.

6.  As a special school, you have outstanding provision for autism, and know that local primaries and secondaries would like to collaborate.

7.  The trust's special educational needs (SEN) hubs in its primary schools are superb, yet to be extended into secondary.

8.  The trust's primary curriculum is excellent, ripe for marketing to schools across the region.

9.  The trust has recently purchased an old school on the coast to turn into a residential centre. The opportunities to market this centre to other schools are enormous.

So how do you build on these achievements for the future?

## SEIZING OPPORTUNITIES

Unlike the executives whose professional lives have the 'urgent consuming the important', their heads rightly focus on the everyday wellbeing and academic progress of pupils – part of the role of governors and trustees is to look outwards. They can lift the school's psyche out of the immediate and help it to see beyond the school gates. Their own contacts and backgrounds can come together to be a powerful force for development and growth rooted in what a school or trust is already very good at.

The key starting point is that whatever mid- and long-term developments are planned, the best interests of the students will be served over time. And that involves creative thinking and meticulous planning in relation to any of the above examples. Governors bring their individual 'expertise' to the table, expertise coming in many guises. Governors remain the guardians of the values and vision of their local school community. Passing fads and fashions are to be eschewed.

Good old 'serendipity' should never be underestimated. Governors might find that just as you are discussing trying to find a partner with whom to expand your sixth form, so too is a school five miles away. What are the possibilities? You want to develop your extensive grounds and you find that the new science park opening next door is looking for a biotech partner. Or you read that the local authority is wanting to expand autism provision, and you can help solve their problem.

The chair and headteacher/CEO will want to ensure – perhaps through an initial strategy day – that there is a collective wish to build on very secure standards and foundations. A board will want to satisfy itself that senior leaders will not take their eyes off the main thing: the student's daily good education. Clearly, a number of board members must be prepared to devote some extra time to first steps as the school/trust look outwards.

****

It is true to observe that across the globe providers of international schools have brought education to the market. Glance at any set of statistics and they tell you that the growth of new fee-paying schools globally is exponential. These are in many cases outstanding education businesses, some rooted in English independent schools.

Government education systems are playing catch-up, looking keenly at what their own state-run systems can learn from the private sector. The past decade in England has seen a greater entrepreneurial spirit in education, partly generated by the multi-academy trust system, partly by school and trust boards recognising that central and local government finances are increasingly squeezed.

'Xenacious' is not an everyday word. It needs to enter every board's vocabulary; that yearning to develop, to think the unthinkable, to dream a little, to look outwards for opportunities to promote great education and enter into partnerships with fellow conspirators. Start now!

Hearts and minds, timing, communication, luck – the 'change cocktail' – each will play its part. And be aware: the problem with the almost tangible future is that the lead-in times are a killer.

# ASIDE

## WHAT TO DO?

An academy trust comprising of just seven primary schools is struggling to fulfil its expansion plans.

It has a school in a different DfE region 50 miles away to where it is headquartered, and that school is starting to fail. It appoints a new governing body just before an inspection puts it into special measures.

The new governing body concludes that the trust lacks the resources to support a turn around and, with the support of the distant trust board, approaches its local regional commissioner for help in brokering to a different trust. The governing body also holds informal discussions with two local trusts.

The regional commissioner's initial reaction is to agree that brokering is desirable and states that the DfE will take the lead. Three months later, there is no apparent action on the part of the DfE and the school is not improving.

*What should the governing body do?. . .*

\*\*\*\*

A successful village primary school has received a series of complaints from two parents about aspects of the curriculum and how it is taught. These have been investigated according to the complaints procedure and have been deemed to be without merit.

The parents have also been publicly rude about the school and its headteacher. The governing body has come to the view that the parents are being vexatious and that their actions are having a detrimental effect — distracting leadership time and affecting the wellbeing of staff.

The parents are informed via a meeting and in writing that the school will not entertain similar complaints, and requests them to desist from making derogatory comments about the headteacher.

The parents do not comply and start making Freedom of Information (FoI) requests of the school, further diverting leadership time and causing more stress.

*What does the governing body do?. . .*

\*\*\*\*

# ZOOM

**Conducting business virtually requires different skillsets.**

As a brand name which entered the international lexicon courtesy of the global pandemic, there can be few bigger winners than Zoom. Its original tagline of 'frictionless communication' gave way to 'one platform delivering limitless human connection' – and the website now proclaims: 'The heart of human connection, dedicated to delivering happiness'.

The Zoom, Teams or Google virtual call has certainly transformed aspects of governance – so many organisations now hold their main board meetings in-person but have moved committee business online. What have been the gains and losses from earlier times?

In schools the legacy of the global pandemic continues. Well-rehearsed is the argument that the extended lockdowns of schools served to widen the disadvantage gap, even though schools stayed open for those students in need of a safe space and continued to deliver increasingly imaginative online learning.

Furthermore, school attendance, especially in secondary schools, has not recovered its pre-Covid levels. Many pundits have talked about 'a breaking of the social contract' so that families no longer see as a given sending their children to school every day. Certainly parents are much more likely to take their children out of school for holidays in term time than was hitherto the case – governors will know the story well.

A companion statistic is the estimated 200,000 children who are electing to be home educated, a number set to increase despite greater government vigilance on the quality of what is being provided at home. This is not just a UK phenomenon, but it is said that this country is the work-from-home capital of Europe, a fact which arguably leads to more children doing the same as their parents on odd days.

In sum, there is no reversing the events and the shift of attitudes towards the workplace and the schoolplace of recent years. We need to harness the transformation and opportunities that the online world can bring.

## ADVANTAGES AND DISADVANTAGES OF THE VIRTUAL

There is nothing new of course about video calls and video conferencing. Global companies and charities have been holding 'partner town-halls' for many years – that is how they have done and still do their high-profile business. It is the advance of technology that means that communicating across time zones and oceans is almost free, a vision Bill Gates articulated back in 1975 at the birth of Microsoft. The once extraordinary has truly become the commonplace in our hyper-connected world.

Research and experience across the country indicate that a large majority of boards' main meetings take place in-person; and a similarly large percentage opt for regular committee meetings online. Schools that serve a tight local community can often secure a greater percentage of in-person meetings; trusts covering a wider geographical reach opt for the virtual. Boards are wise to keep their arrangements under annual review, adjusting according to members' preferences and experiences.

A number of identified advantages of the virtual meeting have emerged through the trials of the past few years, though there is not a consensus on these matters. Personal, subjective preferences tend to trump objective research on the topic. On the plus side, voices articulate:

1. In busy lives today, not having to travel far to meetings is a real boon, for personal and professional reasons.
2. Meetings begin and end on time. They have to. If you blink, you miss them. And if governors know they have the meeting scheduled in their diary, they will switch on at the right moment. Thus, overall attendance has improved.
3. Meetings tend to be shorter and more focused. We have just an hour, so let's make those 60 minutes count.

4. Those governors who are perhaps shy to speak in meetings can engage through the chat function – and then be invited by the chair to develop a point they have made. (This engagement of shy students was a notable feature during the schools' lockdowns.)

And on the minus side, this critique surfaces:

1. Connectivity is an issue – nothing worse than a meeting punctuated by poor IT connections.

2. One or two voices can dominate if allowed to, and there is not enough exchange of opinions.

3. Screen exchanges are imperfect: the richness of in-person discussion is missed.

4. You come away from meetings wondering whether justice has been done to a topic.

Arguably, in-person meetings have improved in their conduct because of the strictures that have become a feature of virtual meetings.

And blended meetings – ones where governors dial in to a largely in-person meeting – get a bit of a thumbs down in questionnaires to governors: 'neither in nor out of the meeting', and difficult for the chair to manage.

## PROTOCOLS

What emerges strongly from interviews about online meetings is that the *protocols* need to be even more firmly enforced than for in-person meetings, identifying in particular:

- Clearly adhered to start and finish times
- Tight agenda, with fixed timings where possible
- Agreed use of 'mute' and 'chat', whatever might suit a smaller or larger group. Ensure all participants are in a 'safe space' at home and no one else can listen in
- Camera must be on 'so we can see the smiles and the whites of each other's eyes'

- Chair's role even more crucial: managing who speaks when, balancing executive input with that of governors.

There are alternative views: the word 'netiquette' is worth googling. And in the words of one chair of governors: 'How many zoom calls have been conducted in bed, in the car, in pyjamas? I have had many zoom calls while walking outside. It's actually amazing how walking and talking stimulates one's creativity and thinking. Why should we be behind a desk?' Discuss.

What also surfaces through conversations with many board members in varied contexts is that there is a broad agreement that the *quality* of decision making around an actual table trumps the virtual roundtable. In our people business, governors feel that the gentle hand gesture, the raised eyebrow, the winning smile – these count very much in affirming the right outcomes.

# CODA

Are all of the above the conclusions of the generation of so-called 'digital refugees'? Do the 'digital natives' and 'digital nomads' instead glimpse a future of online meetings only.

One CEO tells the delightful tale that her trust recently decided to open two nurseries in a town, the start potentially of an ambitious programme to ensure that in their community truly 'no child will be left out or left behind'. Her trust board are passionate believers in such a vision.

The first child registered to join one of the nurseries was called Hope. What auspicious beginnings! What is true is that governors when visiting children in nurseries today can look at those children and know they will likely live towards the year 2125, by when the currently titled GRIN technologies – genetics, robotics, internet, nanotechnology – will have advanced in ways undreamt of today.

We can debate whether humans will command the machines, or the other way round. We can debate, as futurologists do, *possible* futures: whether blindness, cancer and dementia will have been eradicated; whether wars, relentless migration of peoples and environmental degradation will fundamentally change our globe. We can debate the comedian's quip: 'I have seen the future, and it's very much like the present, only longer.'

Might we affirm a *probable* future that the place called school will still exist, in-person or in Zoomland?

---

# ASIDE

## WHAT TO DO?

A governing board has asked repeatedly to see data about pupil performance and attendance. The headteacher has given broad headlines but says it is too difficult to get data for every year group or for specific characteristics of pupil — and anyway 'the only thing that's important are the headline figures'.

No other member of the senior leadership team ever attends board meetings and so the only source of information comes from the headteacher. A couple of vocal governors demand change.

*How should the board tackle this?. . .*

\*\*\*\*

One parent member of the governing board (a former teacher) has enthusiastically taken up the governance responsibility for teaching and learning. She has started going into lessons, looking through students' books and making notes and comments which have upset staff.

What she has reported back to governors — in quite a provocative style — has some merit.

The headteacher has had a long history of difficulty with this particular parent and is reluctant to address the issue themselves. The governing body has been asked to deal with this situation.

*What is the plan of action?. . .*

\*\*\*\*

# YOUTH

### Successful boards ensure wise succession planning.

We are not talking just chronological age here, yet it remains the case that the majority of governing boards do not have many members under the age of 40 amongst their number. If this is not too provocative a suggestion, look around your own board: is the average age below 50? Given that the average life expectancy in the UK today nudges 82 years, that may be fine.

In the long-running, highly popular film series *Succession*, the intrigues, jealousies, plotting, twists and surprise denouements are the stuff of fiction – or, if you believe certain voices, it's all based on the long-running saga of Rupert Murdoch's family empire.

Fact or fiction, the series is focused on that vital subject for any thriving organisation: successful succession, the passing on of an undimmed torch to the next generation of youthful spirits.

One of the great joys of working in schools – and why people do it for a lifetime – is seeing the growth and development of children and young people, their acquisition of new skills and knowledge, their constant questioning with why, how, where, when?

I assert that the best teachers remain 'children at heart'. They can be both childlike and childish, at the right times. To borrow from the great lines of J. M. Barrie in *Peter and Wendy*: 'On these magic shores children at play are for ever beaching their coracles. We too have been there; we can still hear the sound of the surf, though we shall land no more' (Barrie, 1911).

Youth of course can get a bad name, as it has through literature and films over many centuries. Youth, they say, is wasted on the young.

Charles Dickens, that great chronicler of Victorian society and shaper of social attitudes to this day, created memorable images of youth in Pip, the Artful Dodger, Oliver Twist, Little Dorrit, David Copperfield and the rest. Shakespeare in *The Winter's Tale* (Shakespeare, 1623) has the Shepherd say: 'I would there were no age between ten and three-and-twenty, or that youth would sleep out the rest, for there is nothing in the between but getting wenches with child, wronging the ancientry, stealing, fighting.'

Philosopher Thomas Hobbes in the 17th century declared that life was 'solitary, poor, nasty, brutish and short' (Hobbes, 1651).

The refrain today is that age is just a number – so be it. We should speak of the young at heart, not chronological age. Yet it should be the ambition of all forward-thinking boards to look at how they are securing the future. Many, many boards *are* deeply reliant on those who have retired from full-time paid employment, who are at a point in their lives where they have time to give back generously to the wider society and to their own communities. Tremendous!

A good number of employers encourage their employees to volunteer their services to schools and charities; others are less generous and insist that volunteering days are taken as part of annual holiday allowance. Given that there are an estimated 300,000+ school/trust governors in the UK, releasing them compulsorily – as with those who are Justices of the Peace – would be a serious requirement of employers.

The combined ages and experiences of any board shape how it works. Wise boards do intermittently take stock and ask members to think about their future intentions and their periods of office. With that knowledge the chair and executive can consider succession planning.

## SUCCESSION PLANNING

First, it is important to look at who is on a board and may wish to stand for a further period of office. Experience, talent and proven commitment already in the room is where to start. In the same way that the workplace in recent years has become more fluid with part-time working and flexible over office attendance (some would say 'too much churn'), so too organisations dependent on volunteers have become more open to new ways of doing.

In teaching, secondments and sabbaticals are not only possible but a growing feature for the profession. Prescient governing boards and trusts continue to think and plan creatively. An interesting version of this is from one of the Australian states wishing to recruit teachers to isolated rural schools: an 80% salary for five years; you teach for four years, the fifth is a sabbatical.

What might secondments and sabbaticals look like on a board if someone requests one, perhaps to spend a term with their family in another country? Or a parent governor may wish to stand down for six months as their Year 13 child needs support through the final year at school. And might the highly valued chair wish to have a 'rest from duties' for a couple of terms, passing over the reins to a keen vice-chair? What better induction for a deputy.

To rule out any of these without fair consideration would not reflect well on an experienced team of governors; encouraging and promoting such approaches, without destabilising, may well be beneficial to sustaining a high performing board.

****

All great organisations talent spot and routinely ask their top performers the question: So who is your apprentice? Who is going to fill your place when you move on?

It is a truism in teaching, and many walks of life besides, that whether a new entrant stays long in their chosen craft, trade or profession – even after investing in initial training – hinges significantly upon the quality of their mentoring.

Ask a plumber, an actuary, a butcher or a secretary whether they were well nurtured in their first year. Ask that question of any Early Career Teacher (ECT) in your school, and they will testify to the importance of that mentoring. In the same way, any new governors thrive when they have a 'buddy' to help them along when they have a question they would prefer not to ask in full audience.

It is increasingly the case as reported by governor associations around the country that, just as with teaching, recruitment and retention gets no easier as the years go by. This needs serious thought by boards. Take the case of the SEND or safeguarding governor. The workload and responsibilities have grown and grown, to the point where many volunteers just do not have the time to do the good job they want to do. Can the roles be shared? How can we do differently?

Board members need to do their own bit of talent spotting so that when a vacancy arises and is advertised, there are likely to be some interested candidates.

## OBSERVERS AND CO-OPTIONS

Many boards bring on fresh blood through welcoming observers from time to time, and co-opting people from the local community to join a committee for a short period of time to help develop a project. Protocols and expectations around governance guidelines and such matters as confidentiality and access to information need to be tight. Once agreed, the added value of such folk can often be immeasurable, bringing different perspectives to the board.

These observers and co-optees may in turn be the governors or trustees of the future, and the clerk will be sure to include them in notifications of training opportunities.

In this context of observers, senior secondary students can bring their vital perspectives to committees and main board meetings. It is common today to see these digital natives informing discussions on AI, social media and the use of technology in classrooms.

## LEGACY

Legacy is not a topic one hears much discussed by boards. Good governance gets on with governing. Boards meet to a timetable, are serviced by their committees and knowing clerks, they do their duty and seek to serve their school communities.

The alpha and the omega of what they do and how they do it has been the substance of this book, from boards and chairs, to housekeeping and minutes, to risks and zoom. Wise governance of our national school system is so very important. To borrow from Dr Samuel Johnson again, we soon know when it is not being well practised.

Overwhelmingly across the county, the volunteer imperative means that integrity, intelligence and commitment underpin the vital oversight and insights which trust and school governing boards deliver.

May good governance be among you.

## ASIDE

### WHAT TO DO?

One of your trustees is considering applying for a senior position that has come available in the trust. She is a highly respected trustee and known for her strong and well-articulated views on a range of topics.

There is nervousness from both chair and CEO about a trustee making this shift of role.

*What steps should the board take to ensure that the process is as transparent and fair as possible?...*

\*\*\*\*

The local advisory group of one of the highly successful schools in the trust (the trust has replaced governing boards with 'advisory groups') wants to have more authority over decisions the school makes.

The advisory group has insisted on meeting regularly with the headteacher, asking for updates and reports on areas that within the scheme of delegation they have no authority over. The headteacher approaches the trust board for advice.

And there are signs from two other schools of similar questioning.

*The board meets to discuss this as a major item...*

\*\*\*\*

# SECTION
# TWO

# SCENARIOS FOR TRAINING AND DISCUSSION: WHAT TO DO?

**1.** During an Ofsted inspection one of the governors discloses information that perhaps was not relevant to the inspection, but has called in question aspects of the strong judgement for leadership and management.

The principal and senior team were able to deal with the situation and reassure the lead inspector, after lengthy discussions.

After the inspection, the principal asks the chair for that governor to be interviewed by their peers and asked why she risked compromising the final judgement.

*The governors take this forward...how?...*

**2.** A primary school board is delighted to have a new and very energetic parent governor elected to join it. She appears very much aligned with the school's aims, goals and ethos, and all looks promising.

Then the focus appears to shift very much to preoccupation with the education her child is receiving. It starts with the odd comment in governors' meetings, and then to vocal criticism of the class teacher, and senior staff, qualified by such comments as, 'I've talked to other parents about this...'.

Next, she starts writing strong letters to the headteacher and, when she considers the replies she receives unsatisfactory, raises a formal complaint. The headteacher feels totally undermined.

*What can the chair and board do next?...*

**3.** The finance and audit committee feels lucky to have attracted a high-powered investment banker on its strength. The audit will be in safe hands, and the school business manager is reassured that she will receive plenty of appropriate support and advice.

It is not long before the business manager complains to the principal and chair that the new governor insists on checking all her accounting practices, and goes through figures with a fine-tooth comb, frequently insisting on doing things differently – 'In my world we would not tolerate that...' – and imposing his own spending priorities, insisting that the board will see things his way.

*What next for the committee and the board?...*

**4.** One of the governors has so many contacts in the local business world that he always seems able to encourage local firms to tender for work at very keen prices. This is a relief to the board as a whole.

When the chair goes to a charity dinner at the local Gold Club, she notes that the same governor is surrounded at both table and bar by, it seems, all the owners of those firms who appear to be paying court to him.

This leaves her feeling uneasy, and wondering who is benefitting most from this relationship – the school, the firms or that governor?

*What should the chair do?...*

**5.** The safeguarding governor is fantastically knowledgeable on the subject, being (conveniently) a much-in-demand lawyer doing a lot of work in family law and SEND.

He is punctilious, and absolutely on top of the small print in policies and procedures. The trouble is, he is exceedingly busy, so is often slow to get back to the SENCO or leadership when they need his advice.

He develops a habit of rushing into school in the last day or two before he has to report to the board, demanding enormous amounts of information, becoming impatient when it is not immediately to hand, and defensive or accusatory when challenged by his fellow governors.

*Can the board find a way of making the most of his skills?...*

**6.** The board congratulates itself on recruiting an HR expert to its number. She is the natural first call for joining appointments panels. Her advice – indeed, insistence – on proper procedures is welcome.

When the school leadership wants to draw up a small shortlist for interview of the few well-qualified applicants for a maths teaching post, who all happen to be male, she insists that they create a more diverse field of candidates. This necessitates omitting the best-qualified and experienced male.

*What do involved governors do?...*

**7.** When a governor offers to lead on safeguarding, it's an unwise chair that declines the offer. Moreover, this is not the first time that the governor in question has been on a school board.

His previous school had suffered a serious failure in safeguarding so, taking responsibility for it at this one, he is determined not to let anything slip. He is all over the paperwork and policies, comes in to meet the SENCO and pastoral leads every couple of weeks and then insists that he will attend the school's various pastoral and SEND team meetings, demanding that agendas be sent to him in advance.

*What does the board decide to do?...*

**8.** You are a headteacher in a multi-academy trust. A trust leader has recently been given responsibility for consolidating the approach to reporting to governors so that all reports are based on the same model, with the intention being to increase the capacity for rapid scrutiny by the trust board. You feel that the new structure is restrictive and focuses on the wrong things. Trying to put the information you want to include into the new format is increasing your workload.

*Who could you discuss this with and what would you hope to achieve?...*

**9.** The CEO has joined a trust where a trustee is also a chair of governors for one of the trust schools. The school is subsequently judged inadequate by Ofsted and leadership at all levels is in urgent need of improvement.

The trust board meets to discuss the Ofsted outcome.

*How does the CEO enable the board to understand that the scheme of delegation must change as there must be a clear separation of duties at all levels of governance?...*

**10.** A trust is struggling to find competent governors to serve on the local school boards. The CEO would like to ask the headteachers of the trust's schools to serve as a chair of governors at a neighbouring trust school.

*What are the benefits and potential pitfalls in introducing this model?...*

# GOOD GOVERNANCE: THE ELEVATOR PITCH

*For those unfamiliar with the popular American phrase, the elevator pitch is a clear, concise, compelling few words with a core message...*

Ambassadors: good governors and trustees are powerful ambassadors for their organisations and communities.

Boards: effective boards skilfully weigh their *oversight* and *insight* roles.

Chair: the professional understanding between the chair and the executive leader is arguably *the* decisive factor in the success of an organisation.

Delegation: practising proper levels of delegation lies at the heart of a thriving governing board.

Executive: knowing where governance ends, and executive practice begins, is a hallmark of the successful board.

Fires: addressing and resolving conflicts and emergencies are true tests of confident governance.

Guests: thoughtful boards know when to look outwards to refresh their established thinking and practices.

Housekeeping: the wise governing body has shared expectations of its own housekeeping rules.

Interviewing: staging and managing high quality interviews of all descriptions lie at the core of strong governance.

Judgements: the wisdom, timing and communication of decision making shapes top governance.

**Knowledge:** the highly respected governing body comprehensively 'knows its onions'.

**Lorenzetti:** vibrant organisations celebrate strong leadership at all levels.

**Minutes:** 'the person who controls the minutes controls the meetings.'

**Nolan:** seven elegant principles of public life worth observing, at every turn.

**Optimism:** optimism radiates from confident school leaders and board chairs.

**People:** capable trustees never lose sight of the fact that they are in the people business.

**Questions:** asking great questions – and listening keenly to the answers – are hallmarks of successful governing boards.

**Risks:** an acute eye on balancing risks is ever on the governance agenda.

**Seneca:** the accomplished board is comfortable in its own skin.

**Training:** time is well spent training a board to be the best it can be.

**Unconventional:** valuing the unorthodox and the maverick is critical to fine governance.

**Volunteers:** motivating a group of volunteers 'to turn up next time' should not be underplayed.

**Walkabout:** engaged boards make time to walk around the 'estate' of the organisation.

**Xenacious:** scanning the horizon for 'what next' distinguishes excellent governance.

**Youth:** successful boards ensure wise succession planning.

**Zoom:** conducting business virtually requires different skillsets.

****

1.  How do you rate yourself as a governor/trustee against these points?
2.  How do you rate your board against these points?
3.  If you were rewriting this book, which A–Z chapter titles would you use?

# GOOD AT...BETTER AT...

This is the summary of responses to a questionnaire completed by members of a governing body, as a starting point for a subsequent board training programme.

*'We are good at...'*

- Quality of communication good as it should be
- Values individual views – on a humanitarian level
- Strong sense of continuity
- Decisions based on facts
- Keeps accurate minutes and records
- Trust in headteacher to manage operational issues
- Provides constructive guidance to SLT
- Adheres well to confidentiality
- Tries to reflect all views of parents, staff and students
- A willingness to accept that things should not just remain the same
- Commitment to explore/investigate issues thoroughly
- Decisions taken in the best interests of students and staff
- Balances well the commercial and operational aspects with student, parent and teacher wellbeing
- Has stepped up during a crisis at short notice when required on multiple issues.

*'We could be better at…'*

- Improve communication
- Adding value between meetings
- Be more solution focused as opposed to highlighting issues
- More active in setting overall goals and policies
- Improved flow between committees and main board
- It's a meeting, not a conversation – focus less on personal agendas
- Have a more strategic outlook, rather than being reactive
- Reviewing the long term 'strategic intents' as outlined by the principal
- We do not seem to measure or communicate our own performance as a board
- Shorter, more focused meetings, even if that means meeting more regularly
- Defining the lines between strategy/board matters and management
- More exposure to the school operations first hand
- Governors need to know how to preserve confidentiality, while conveying agreed public messages
- A clearer view on roles and responsibilities of principal, chair and governors – leading to a code of conduct for the board.

****

1. What would a similar review of your board identify?
2. What is your board good and very good at?
3. What do you think your board might wish to be better at?

# GOVERNANCE REVIEW RECOMMENDATIONS

The following is a list of recommendations made to a board of governors.

- Continue to build in opportunities for governors, including new governors, to network informally, familiarise themselves with each other's background and skills, and form an effective team.
- Review the timing of meetings, perhaps holding some early in the morning or after normal working hours.
- Undertake an up-to-date skills audit and endeavour to address gaps in future governor recruitment. Where this is not practicable or in the shorter term, address gaps where necessary by co-option or by identifying sources of expertise on which to draw.
- While always seeking the best person for the role, ensure through appropriate advertising and communication that a diverse range of potential candidates are encouraged to apply for governor positions.
- Implement the new systematic, structured induction process for new governors and for any who would value a 'refresher', review its effectiveness, and ensure a proportionate approach to training.
- Establish an evaluation process for the board both individually and collectively, and schedule the necessary dates in an annual calendar of governor business.
- Periodically seek feedback from governors on the content, style and level of detail of the information provided for board meetings. Consider the use of infographics to present data as clearly and concisely as possible.
- Chair to ensure a balance of input among governors, and to seek to ensure positions taken are supported by sound information.

- Remind trustees of the importance of identifying possible conflicts of interest and adopt an 'if in doubt, declare' approach.
- Introduce an annual 'awayday' to allow for longer term issues to be considered separately from routine business, and also improve board cohesion.
- Arrange a periodic opportunity for board members to meet a wide range of staff to explain their role and ensure such an explanation forms part of staff induction.

****

1. Which of these might ring true as recommendations to your board?
2. What action would you like to see your board take to further improve its work?
3. What is the best practice you have seen with boards which your board is not currently doing?

# CODE OF CONDUCT: GOVERNORS' MUTUAL EXPECTATIONS

## FULFIL OUR ROLE & RESPONSIBILITIES

1. I accept that my role is strategic and so will focus on our core functions rather than involve myself in day-to-day management of the school.

2. I will develop, share and live the ethos and values of our school.

3. I agree to adhere to school policies and procedures as set out by the relevant governing documents.

4. I will work collectively for the benefit of the school.

5. I will be candid yet constructive and respectful in discussions with senior leaders and board members.

6. I will consider how our decisions may affect the students, staff, parents and the wider local community.

7. I will stand by the decisions that we make as a collective board.

8. I will only speak or act on behalf of the board if I have the authority to do so.

9. I will act fairly and without prejudice.

10. I will follow the established procedures when making or responding to complaints.

11. I will not bring complaints from parents or staff to the board, but will direct the complainant to the relevant school procedure. However, I will be a voice for the entire school community.

12. I will uphold the school's reputation in my private communications, including in discussions with parents and on social media.

## DEMONSTRATE OUR COMMITMENT TO THE ROLE

1. I will involve myself actively in the work of the board, and accept my fair share of responsibilities, serving on committees or working groups where required.

2. I will make every effort to attend all meetings, and where I cannot attend, I will explain in advance why I am unable to attend.

3. I will arrive at meetings prepared, having read all papers in advance, ready to make a positive contribution and observe protocol.

4. I will get to know the school well and respond to opportunities to involve myself in school activities.

5. When visiting the school in a personal capacity (i.e. as a parent or carer), I will continue to honour these commitments.

## BUILD AND MAINTAIN RELATIONSHIPS

1. I will develop effective working relationships with school leaders, staff, parents and other relevant stakeholders from our local community.

2. I will express views openly, courteously and respectfully in all our communications with board members and staff, both inside and outside of meetings.

3. I will support the chair in their role of leading the board and the principal in their role of leading the school, ensuring appropriate conduct at all times.

## RESPECT CONFIDENTIALITY

1. I will observe complete confidentiality both inside and outside of school when matters are deemed confidential or where they concern individual staff, pupils or families.

2. I will not reveal the details of any governing board vote, discussion, report, paper or any other matters that are part of the board's work, whether it is discussed at board, committee meetings or elsewhere.

3. I will ensure all confidential papers are held and disposed of appropriately.

4. I will maintain confidentiality even after I leave office.

## DECLARE CONFLICTS OF INTEREST AND BE TRANSPARENT

1. I will declare any business, personal or other interest that I have in connection with the board's business and these will be recorded in the Register of Business Interests held by the honorary secretary.

2. I will also declare any conflict of loyalty at the start of any meeting should the need arise.

3. If a conflicted matter arises in a meeting, I will leave the meeting for the duration of the discussion and any subsequent vote.

4. I will act in the best interests of the school as a whole and not as a representative of any individual or group.

5. I accept that in the interests of open governance, our full names, dates of appointment, terms of office, roles on the governing board, relevant business and pecuniary interests, and category of governor will be published on the school's website.

I understand that potential or perceived breaches of this code will be taken seriously and that a breach could lead to formal sanctions.

| Signed | Name | Date |
|---|---|---|
| | | |

The governing board agree that this code of conduct will be reviewed annually, upon significant changes to the law and policy or as needed, and it will be endorsed by the full governing board.

****

What is your analysis of these headings and the individual points?

1. What do you see as the merits or shortcomings of such a charter, signed by governors?

2. What similar kind of charter exists where you are a governor or trustee?

# GOVERNOR TRAINING EXERCISES

## PART 1

Governors, by definition, bring a wide range of experiences and backgrounds to the board. Training therefore needs to avoid being one-size-fits-all.

That said, given where the board is, and building on previous training, it might be useful to focus on four points in the best interests of new and longer-standing governors:

1. What is our shared understanding of 'confidentiality' and of the crucial line between operational and strategic?

2. What do we mean when we talk about 'excellent communication' between ourselves, and between the board members and the executive team?

3. How can we be effective in setting strategic objectives for our school? How do we see education 2025-32?

4. What key performance indicators should we set ourselves as a board? And should we produce an annual report (digital) about the board's work?

****

## PART 2

The following bullets are taken from published review and inspection reports about governance in schools in the UK and internationally.

A useful training exercise is to take each of these for discussion and ask:

*What would we wish to see written about governance at our school?*

- The board has ensured clarity of vision, ethos and strategic direction through regular reviews of its work, refreshing its vision and values following a commissioned external review. Furthermore, the board has driven implementation through performance management and the refreshed scheme of delegation.

- The board holds executive leaders to account through board-led meetings, including non-executive only sessions at each meeting. It has established a standards committee with its membership, including senior leaders from other trusts, to ensure an additional layer of rigour in scrutinising performance.

- The board uses external advice to support its review of the performance of the chief executive, and the trust's remuneration committee reviews the performance of all those who report to the chief executive.

- The board oversees the financial performance of the organisation at every board meeting and through its finance and audit committee and risk committee. Its board members have significant experience and expertise and have overseen the move from a deficit in the 2023 accounts of over £1 million to building a healthier reserve.

- The board ensures compliance through its routine scrutiny of the executive's work, through the reporting of all internal and external reviews to the board, including health and safety and safeguarding, and through the internal and external audits it commissions.

- The board is restless to develop and improve its practices. It has a passion for the improvement of the trust schools and for the achievement of every pupil. It is most concerned about excellent governance.

- The board invites to all its meetings an external adviser (a) to support it on the key education matters it considers, and (b) to comment on its own effectiveness. The trust's own governance professional is a National Leader of Governance.

****

# GOVERNORS' VISITS TO SCHOOLS: THE PROTOCOL

## CONTEXT

One of the key roles and responsibilities for the governing body is to monitor the progress and performance of the school. Undertaking visits demonstrates the governors' role in the strategic management of the school by helping to hold the school to account and evaluate its progress.

The governors' visiting programme is an integral part of the school's yearly monitoring calendar. A governor is encouraged to make at least two visits a year during school time, and governors will often monitor an area of the school strategic plan.

Visits enable governors to:

- See the school at work and observe the range of attitudes, behaviour and achievements
- Get to know the staff and demonstrate their commitment to the school
- Give active support to the staff and the activities of the school
- Be aware of the effect of change and different approaches to teaching and learning
- Evaluate resources and discuss with staff further requirements
- Gain first-hand information to assist with policy making and decision taking
- Work in partnership with the staff.

Before making a visit governors will:

- Contact the principal and agree a date, time and focus for the visit

- Clarify the etiquette, courtesies and expectations for the visit
- Plan which classes will be visited
- Draw up a timetable for the visit with the assistant principal or subject coordinator

*Assistant principal and/or the subject coordinator ensure that all staff are aware of the visit and the expectations on them.*

On the day of the visit the governor will remember to:

- Arrive on time and clarify the timetable with the assistant principal/ subject coordinator
- Act as an observer and only participate in the class at the invitation of the teacher
- Respect the professionalism of the teacher, supporting but not interfering
- Be calm and enjoy the visit.

After the visit the governor will:

- Remember to thank the teachers and children
- Meet with the principal to give a verbal report, and to raise any issues that arose

*Governors should not report on individual students and staff.*

It is important to remember that visits are a snapshot in time, and judgements should not be made arbitrarily. *The visit is not about:*

- Inspection
- Making judgements about the professional expertise of the teacher
- Checking on your own children
- Pursuing a personal agenda
- Arriving with inflexible pre-conceived ideas

*Governors need to be mindful of confidentiality issues and will not discuss the visits outside the governing body.*

## REFLECTION

How might visits contribute to the **strategic thinking** of the governing body?

- What are we seeing in classrooms that gives us ideas about what Education 2035 might look like, for different age groups?
- What do we see and hear that informs our future thinking about investments in different parts of the school?
- What do we observe that helps us evaluate the impact of the governing board?

# ROLE OF GOVERNING BODY WITHIN A TRUST

## THE ROLE OF THE LOCAL GOVERNING BODY

The governors exercise the responsibilities and duties delegated by the trust board as set out in the scheme of delegation (an example scheme of delegation is available on the Unity Schools Partnership website).

The local governing body will set the vision and strategic direction for the school so that it is appropriate for the context of the school and for the local community, and includes implementing the vision of the trust board and its objectives. The local governing body is the ears and eyes of the trust in the community that the school serves and ensures that the education delivered is appropriate for that community.

Each governor will familiarise themselves with the scheme of delegation and ensure that the local governing body carries out its delegated functions as specified in the scheme.

## 2.2.1 GOVERNORS ARE RESPONSIBLE FOR

**STRATEGIC DIRECTION**: Ensuring the trust's and school's visions, values and ethos are realised.

Governors

- oversee the implementation of the Board's strategy as it applies to the school
- with the Headteacher, are responsible for developing the school's strategic plan
- with the Headteacher, oversee the development and regular updating of the school's Development/Improvement Plan, based on accurate self-evaluation
- contribute to priorities, including the suitability of the staffing structure within the final budget and 3-year forecast
- understand and evaluate the impact of restricted funds
- ensure pupil premium/sports premium and catch-up funds are being spent appropriately
- review the opportunities for revenue generation

**SAFEGUARDING & WELLBEING:** Putting our pupils, staff and community at the heart of what we do.

Governors

- are responsible for knowing and understanding the school's own evaluation of the quality of spiritual, moral, social and cultural development of pupils
- monitor, support and challenge the welfare and child protection processes in the school including attendance, behaviour, serious disciplinary incidents and exclusions
- appoint a link governor to oversee the board's work on safeguarding

**CHALLENGE & SUPPORT**: Through monitoring, dialogue and stakeholder engagement.

Governors

- support the school in its self-evaluation of significant strengths and weaknesses, including the school's own evaluation of the quality of teaching
- support and challenge the school in its programme of improvement
- are responsible for knowing, understanding and challenging the provisions that are in place to support pupils' progress and attainment, including for different groups of pupils
- challenge and advise the school in the development and implementation of its curriculum policy and, where appropriate, qualifications policy
- appoint link governors to have specific responsibility for pupils with Special Needs; pupils who attract Pupil Premium funding and Looked After Children and who report to the full Local Governing Body (LGB) as appropriate
- in secondary schools, appoint a link governor with responsibility for Careers
- in primary schools, are responsible for monitoring the school's evaluation of the quality of EYFS provision
- are responsible for monitoring the school's links with, and provision of information to, parents, carers, guardians and the wider community
- ensure that regular surveys of staff, parents and children are carried out to determine their experiences and opinions and to discuss any actions taken by the school as a result of these

**COMPLIANCE & EFFECTIVENESS**: Ensuring adherence to trust, school and statutory policy and guidance.

Governors

- ensure adherence to the regular cycle of school policy reviews
- note trust wide policies and their implications for the school
- ensure compliance with Public Sector Equality Duty requirements for schools

- handle and monitor complaints
- understand the requirements of the inspection process, support the Headteacher and engage fully with that process when it happens
- with the designated trust lead, review GDPR compliance
- are responsible for knowing and understanding training requirements for safer recruitment, including for LGB members
- understand the training requirements for safer recruitment and support the Headteacher by joining appointment panels for senior leadership posts as required or otherwise by contributing to the process
- monitor, support and challenge the health and safety performance at the school
- monitor the impact of the strategic plan on the quality of the school's buildings, including developing priorities for capital expenditure and large scale 'minor works' in line with the strategic plan
- oversee risk management at the local level, including regular reviews of the school's risk register
- approve 'Type 2' educational visits.

# TRUSTEE/GOVERNOR REFLECTION FORM

| Name | | Date appointed | |
|---|---|---|---|
| **What do I do that makes me an effective trustee/governor?** | **Scale 1-5**<br>(5 = excellent) | **Comments** | |
| I actively support our school/trust vision, mission, values and strategic direction | | | |
| I understand my legal responsibilities | | | |
| I attend board/committee meetings regularly | | | |
| I come to meetings well prepared, having read all papers | | | |
| I ask relevant and constructive questions | | | |
| I share my opinion and explain my thinking openly | | | |
| I make it easy for others to share thoughts and opinions or ask difficult questions | | | |
| I listen and learn from others' experience on the board | | | |
| I spend time getting to know the executive and other board members | | | |
| I am a positive ambassador within my networks | | | |
| I provide support and challenge to the executive team to enable them to be effective leaders | | | |
| I feel the chair adds value in their role and performs their role in accordance with the organisation's values | | | |
| I have found induction effective [if you have had an induction over the last 12 months] | | | |
| | | | |

| What have I learned from my experience as a trustee/governor in the past 12 months? |
| --- |
| |
| **What areas would I like to develop in my role over the next 12 months?** |
| |
| **What do I need from my fellow board/committee members and from the executive to help me be the most effective trustee/governor I can be?** |
| |

# AN EXTERNAL REVIEWER'S AGENDA FOR MEETING TRUSTEES

## AGENDA FOR TRUSTEE DISCUSSIONS

1. Welcome & Purpose of the Meeting

   - Overview of the review scope
   - Expected outcomes of the discussion

2. Governance Structure & Decision Making

   - How effectively does the current governance model support **long-term strategic planning**?
   - Are there areas where **board oversight** is insufficient or overly complex?
   - Do you believe **local governance structures** are well-aligned with trust priorities? If not, what changes should be considered?
   - Should a **dedicated committee** be established for trust-wide outreach and professional development?

3. Leadership & Staffing Structure

   - From your perspective, does the current **executive leadership structure** provide the right level of capacity for growth?
   - Do you think creating a **second deputy CEO (education & school improvement)** would strengthen trust leadership?
   - Are there particular **roles/functions** you think need greater investment or restructuring (e.g. digital strategy, external partnerships)?
   - How should the **board's role evolve** in leadership succession planning?

4. Future Growth & Sustainability

- Given recent trust expansion, do you believe the trust should **continue to grow**, or should it consolidate and focus on improvement?
- What **risks and challenges** do you foresee with a more complex governance and staffing structure?
- How can we ensure **greater transparency and accountability** in trust-wide decision making?

5. Closing & Next Steps

- Summary of key discussion points and themes
- Next steps

\*\*\*\*

# REFERENCES

Barrie, J.M. (1911). *Peter and Wendy*. UK: Hodder & Stoughton.

Blatchford, R. (2014). *The Restless School*. Woodbridge: John Catt Educational Ltd.

Blatchford, R. (2023). *The A–Z of Great Classrooms*. Woodbridge: John Catt Educational Ltd.

Blinks Education (2025). 'A Guide to Blinks'. Available at: www.blinks.education/downloads/Guide/GuideToBlinks.pdf

Chesterton, G.K. (1910). *What's Wrong with the World*.

Committee on Standards in Public Life (1995). 'Summary of the Nolan Committee's First Report on Standards in Public Life'. Available at: https://assets.publishing.service.gov.uk/media/5a7da2ed40f0b635051 d0604/1stInquiry_Summary.pdf

Cummings, E.E. (1955). 'A Poet's Advice to Students', *Ottawa Hills High School Spectator*.

De Retz, J.F.P. (1717). Memoirs of Cardinal De Retz

Department for Education (2024). 'Keeping children safe in education 2024'. Available at: https://assets.publishing.service.gov.uk/media/66d7301b9084b18b95709f75/Keeping_children_safe_in_education_2024.pdf

Dickens, C. (1850). *David Copperfield*. UK: Bradbury & Evans.

Education and Skills Funding Agency (2024). 'Academy trust handbook 2024'. Available at: https://assets.publishing.service.gov.uk/media/66a3909aab418ab055592dda/Academy_trust_handbook_2024_FINAL.pdf

Frost, R. (1930). 'The Black Cottage' in *The Collected Poems of Robert Frost*. New York: Henry Holt and Company.

Hartley, L.P. (1953). *The Go-Between*. London: Hamish Hamilton.

Hobbes, T. (1651). *Leviathan or The Matter, Forme and Power of a Commonwealth Ecclesiasticall and Civil.*

Kipling, R. (1910). *Rewards and Fairies.*

McEwan, I. (2014). *The Children Act.* London: Jonathan Cape.

McLuhan, M. (1964). *Understanding Media: The Extensions of Man.* New York: McGraw-Hill.

Neville, S. (2024). 'Veteran Morrisons founder hits out at the board: "Your strategy is a load of bull"', *Independent*, 6 June 2024. Available at: www.independent.co.uk/news/business/news/veteran-morrisons-founder-hits-out-at-the-board-your-strategy-is-a-load-of-bull-9497648.html

Ofsted, Available at: https://reports.ofsted.gov.uk/

Pope, A. (1711). *An Essay on Criticism.* London: W. Lewis.

Rathbone, JP. (2024). 'General Sir Mike Jackson, 1944-2024', *Financial Times*, 16 October. Available at: www.ft.com/content/dc4e2b30-08ca-4bfe-b37f-dda1b5b75ee2

Shakespeare, W. (1623). *The Winter's Tale*, published in the First Folio.

Shaw, G.B. (1903). *Man and Superman.*

Shultz, H. (1999). *Pour Your Heart Into It: How Starbucks Built a Company One Cup at a Time.* New York: Hachette.

Thomas, D. (1954). *A Child's Christmas in Wales.* New Directions.

Vance Marshall, J. (1959). *Walkabout.* UK: Michael Joseph.

# ACKNOWLEDGEMENTS

St Christopher's School, Bahrain

Unity Schools Partnership

Speech and Language UK

Special thanks to: Lisa Taylor, Nick Tate, Keith Grainger, Ian Wilson, Nabila Jiwa, Clare Kershaw and Kate Dethridge.

## OTHER TITLES BY ROY BLATCHFORD

**Roy Blatchford can be contacted via www.blinks.education or at royb88@gmail.com.**

\*\*\*\*

The A-Z series focuses on the 'fun and fundamentals' of what's happening in primary, special and secondary schools today. Each title is written by a leading practitioner, adopting a series approach of reflection, advice and provocation.

As a group of authors with a strong belief in the power of education to shape and change young people's lives, we hope teachers and leaders in the UK and internationally enjoy what we have to say.

**Roy Blatchford, series editor**